Enterprise
On Canvas

A Travelling Post Office on the move
Oil on canvas, 24"×36"

Enterprise On Canvas

Published in association with the
Confederation of British Industry

CBI

ben maile

Q
Quiller Press
LONDON

Also by Ben Maile
THE WORLD, A CANVAS

My affectionate gratitude to Maggie for her patience in translating my handwritten indecipherable notes into legible manuscript.

*S*ometimes we can all get too close to the screen. Those working day by day inside British industry and commerce know that in recent years there has been astounding achievement and progress.

For those who rely for their information on what they read or what they pick up second hand, this quantum leap may not be so apparent.

That was why the Confederation of British Industry, representing a very wide range of manufacturing and service companies, invited artist Ben Maile to take his sketchbook round the country and give an artist's eye view of the changes he found. There was no way that Maile could capture it all. If he painted and sketched for five years he would not be able to put down on canvas all the changes and new drive he discovered in British enterprise, but he has certainly captured the flavour of it. As Britain's Business Voice the CBI is proud to have been associated with the project.

First published in 1987 by
Quiller Press Ltd
50 Albemarle Street, London W1X 4BD

Text and illustrations copyright
© Ben Maile 1987

ISBN 0 907621 90 2

Produced by Hugh Tempest-Radford and
The Five Castles Press Limited, Ipswich.

Set in Century Old Style
by Delafield Reprographics,
2 Weald Road, Brentwood,
Essex CM14 4SX
Printed in Great Britain by
The Ancient House Press, Ipswich

Contents

7   *Foreword* by Sir David Nickson KBE, DL,
President of the Confederation of British Industry

9   *Introduction*

11   *A Global Communications System*
British Telecom International

15   *Electric Mountain*
The Central Electricity Generating Board

21   *The Best Car in the World*
Rolls-Royce Motor Cars

27   *Defence of the Realm*
Vickers Defence Systems

32   *To Penicillin – and Beyond*
The Beecham Group

37   *Dounreay – The Nuclear Future*
UK Atomic Energy Authority

42   *A Nobel Enterprise*
Imperial Chemical Industries

49   *Rulers of the Waves*
Vickers Shipbuilding & Engineering

52   *Spreading the Word on a Grand Scale*
The Post Office and British Rail

59   *Bell, Book and Cable*
British Telecom

62   *A Metalsome Industrial Giant*
The British Steel Corporation

72   *Selby, The New Face of Coal*
British Coal

80   *High-flying Enterprises*
British Aerospace

83   *A Sonic Boom To Success*
British Airways

88 *The Cream of Cornish Industry*
English China Clays

94 *Down The Hatch and Round The Horn*
Whitbread & Co

98 *Britain's Invisible Asset*
British Gas

102 *Printers' Suppliers Par Excellence*
Howson-Algraphy

105 *An Industry of The Utmost Refinement*
British Petroleum

112 *The Big Cat*
Jaguar Cars

115 *The Pinnacle of Finance*
National Westminster Bank

119 *Acorns*
A. & A. Sprinklers

122 George Jowitt & Sons

125 *In The Picture*

128 *Appendix*

Foreword

by Sir David Nickson KBE DL, President of the Confederation of British Industry

*I*t's said that a picture is worth a thousand words. There are times, however, when a picture is worth many thousands of words, more than could usefully be written by the most prolific author and, yet, at the same time, more illuminating than the most crafted poetry. This is one of them. Ben Maile evokes a response which is beyond most of us to express in words.

As President of the Confederation of British Industry I have the opportunity to visit the factories, plants and offices of CBI members across the country. Put down on paper beforehand, this necessitates a daunting itinerary. Actually doing it, however, is a different matter. One is continually surprised at how different the reality is from one's previous conceptions. Even for someone who has been involved in business all their life the technologies demanded by the high-tech age often mean one is exploring a new country: the impressions, the images, the colours, the new skills required – and, above all, the people – need to be witnessed at first hand.

The great engineering feats of the Victorians, so well chronicled, are impressive enough in the illustrations which have come down to us, apart from the reality which is still part of our inheritance. I can say, from my own tours, that equally amazing things are going on now, as industry once again adapts to a changing world. People should be more aware of the excitement of industry, the human commitment which it demands, and the rewards as well as undoubted penalties it involves. Ben Maile, in these canvases, gives the imagination a chance to ponder these things. This chance should be available to a wider audience. At the CBI, we intend to find ways of bringing Ben Maile's vision of industry to young people so that they can appreciate the achievements and the failures of industry in the past and yet not turn away from the challenges of the future.

David Nickson

Introduction

*O*ver the years I have enjoyed some interesting commissions to portray such scenes as mining (coal and china clay), oil platforms in the North Sea and shipping, but to be invited by the CBI to open whatever doors onto industry I cared to choose and view them with a painter's eye was the most challenging and exciting invitation one could wish for.

I started on the project captured mainly by the prospect of recording on paper and canvas the many diverse scenes I knew I was going to see. What painter could not fail to be excited at the sight of a giant blast furnace? What a challenge there is in the vast bulk of one of Her Majesty's submarines sliding into the water on its launching! And there is nothing more likely to concentrate the senses than following, with pencil and sketchbook, the meticulous and intense actions of a Rolls-Royce engine fitter.

To savour fully the visual aspect of any commission the painter needs to know and understand something of his subject, to 'feel and smell' its substance in order to portray it on canvas. Every opportunity was given me to do just that. My senses worked overtime on the shocks, the splendour and the achievements and when the visual appetite was sated I became increasingly aware of the role in all this that mattered most, the role played by man. Through all its changes – and there have been many – in the last decade or two, British industry's workforce has adapted and readapted. Meeting that workforce, talking to them as individuals, sharing a cuppa, watching them as craftsmen at work (a privilege) or as production teams I found my old cynicism dying away. My primary task, the painting, was a great thrill in its doing and, I hope, reflects the scenes I beheld and conveys something of that feel and that smell.

The text is not intended just to substantiate the illustrations, but seeks to portray some of those other vital elements – the historical and the human. Someone needs to knock old prejudices on the head. I saw a broad pattern of success in British industry, a success rate that has put it well up near the top in the international ratings. There have been vast technological advances to aid those successes but without one other factor the technology, no matter how good, would have achieved nothing. That other factor is of course the human one: the British worker who *has* dedication, who *does* take a pride in his work and *is* loyal to his product, and a management more caring, more professional and more committed, both sharing a common work ethic, sheer enterprise.

ben maile

THE MENHIR OR STANDING TREE

Cornwall has many such megaliths. Historians and archaeologists can only debate upon what purpose they might have served to primitive man thousands of years ago. To stand by the mysterious, passive bulk of this stone looking at Goonhilly's satellite aerial a few hundred yards away is to have the imagination fired by outlandish suppositions.
Watercolour, 19" × 15"

A Global Communications System

BRITISH TELECOM INTERNATIONAL

Modern communications begin where the land finishes. At the Lizard, where the southwest corner of our island climbs, starkly dramatic, from the deeps of the Atlantic ocean, modern man built the first radio communications station.

In 1901 Marconi built the (then) world's largest wireless transmitter on the bleak cliffside site of Poldhu. The initial result was puny, a mere 'dit dit dit' – the Morse letter S – but when received the other side of the ocean in Newfoundland the effect worldwide was revolutionary. Radio communication was born.

Sixty-one years later, the Post Office in 1962 built Britain's first earth satellite station at Goonhilly, a comfortable ramble away from Poldhu where it all started.

We know about Goonhilly's 'historic' beginnings with Marconi in 1901 – but what about Ug (or it may have been Og) in 3001 BC? Who? When? Pre-Stone-Age man is who, and his handicraft, between four and six thousand years old, is still standing and authenticated as evidence and proof of Ug's (what's in a name?) existence at Goonhilly in that age. It was evidence that excited me and provoked my – admittedly romantic – imagination, the evidence being a colossal stone megalith, a standing stone or 'menhir' (standing tree). The 15-ton, 15-foot high chunk of gabbro stone is one of many similar megaliths found all over Cornwall. Historians and archaeologists, whilst able accurately to date them have, as yet, found no common answer to the question of their usage. Whether they are significant of some pagan religion or just a signpost is open to debate. Personally, I prefer the image of Ug (the tribe's navigator ?) taking a sight over the great stone on Castor or Pollux.

What would he think now of his menhir's replacements, those great 100-feet dish aerials, sighting, not on Castor or Pollux, or indeed on any heavenly body, but on Intelsat V? Could he ever believe that the bright glowing star above was made and projected into space orbit by his descendants?

Telstar, the first of these man-made satellites, has long since disappeared, fragmented into outer space. Telstar's successors, each one a bewildering complex of Space Age high technology, have created a fantastic network of telephonic and televisual communications right around the globe.

The heart and lungs and arterial system of Goonhilly is housed in small quiet buildings of modest design. Power plants, controls, monitor screens, high voltage cables and waveguides are tucked

away out of sight. The great dishes, dwarfing the ground units, are
just the receiving and transmitting aerials, but they do of course
dominate the scene. At night they assume further stature and
significance. From a distance, silhouetted against a night sky, they
lose all recognisable signs of modernity and become themselves
prehistoric monsters. I look across at the stone menhir. If we play
visual tricks with that too, time itself seems to lose its meaning. But
the ancient enchantment of night is playing no tricks, merely
adding lustre to the wildlife of Goonhilly. The imagined monsters
we know are manmade structures. The startling yet recognisable
cry heard at dusk is no prehistoric creature, it is the tawny owl. Like
many other birds of prey, the owl enjoys a far safer and far more
natural way of life in the Goonhilly complex than many of his fellow
creatures outside the area.

In fact, all wildlife thrives on the site of one of the most advanced
technological units in the country. Paradoxical? Not at all. You see,
the earth satellite station is both noiseless and pollution free. How
dearly would some industries like to list those two qualifications on
their CVs! Once all these important facts had dispelled parochial
fears and suspicions, local management, commendably, went out of
its way to prove that modern science could care, that it could live
equably with the environment, and that its caring extended to
matters of cost and provision. Goonhilly's management not only
pacified and repaired, they improved. Their improvement was such

Goonhilly at dusk
Watercolour, 15" × 22"

ONE OF GOONHILLY'S MASSIVE
SATELLITE AERIALS
These great discs have become part
of the accepted landscape of
southwest Cornwall yet never fail to
startle with dramatic impact, when a
hilltop arrival suddenly presents them
on a sun-streaked horizon.
Watercolour, 30" × 22"

that the local environment and ecology benefited because of the
satellite station.

For myself, I had stated that when I embarked upon this book
I would try and link one particular theme right through – that of
conservation and ecology, in the positive sense of course. I had my
doubts, I admit, but Goonhilly proved to be a surprising and
promising start to that theme.

ELECTRIC MOUNTAIN'S MAIN
INLET VALVE OPERATING
I spent nearly an hour, totally alone,
at this scene, sketching and waiting
for one of the giant valves to function.
When, with an immense sigh of
hydraulic power, the counterbalanced
valve arms swung open, the vibration
was greater than the noise as
thousands of gallons of water surged
past just beneath me. If anything it
heightened the drama of being the
only puny human being viewing that
Wellsian stage of industrial drama.
Oil on canvas, 24"×30"

Electric Mountain

*E*lectricity, the most widely used natural force, is also a *moving* force. It cannot be stored – well, there are limitations. Such batteries as we have so far designed can store only relatively tiny amounts of electricity. Even then these batteries, with the electrons constantly transferring from one plate to another, are always in need of charging. An average car battery at its peak might deliver 60-75 watts. The business and domestic requirements for our nation are measured in terms of thousands of *megawatts* per region. While we literally cannot store electricity in those amounts, with a hydro-electric scheme we can *effectively* store the power insofar that the water supply used for the driving power is stored or held back for re-use. Such a scheme is Dinorwig, or to give it a more magical name 'Electric Mountain'.

If awards were given for advancements in conservation then the Central Electricity Generating Board must be well in line for a medal.

They were faced with the urgent need for back-up supply to the National Grid, to cater for those moments when 10 million heaters go on at peak time in a cold spell, or 18 million *Coronation Street* viewers all switch from telly to cuppa when the first commercial break starts. Something equivalent to about three Battersea power stations would have done. But there weren't any spare power stations lying idle, so they had to build one – but one with a difference.

Their engineers went to Snowdonia, a National Parks area of outstanding beauty. With natural water (lakes) to hand on two different levels, they designed a system that used Newton's famous theory, and at the same time virtually disproved it. In doing so they constructed the biggest subterranean hydro electric plant in existence – and yet visitors to the site can be totally unaware of this phenomenon. The two beautiful lakes – one nearly 2,000 feet above sea level, the other 1,500 feet lower – which provide the catalyst for the power are much as they were, just a little bigger. The scars on Mount Elidir, which houses the whole scheme, are now healed and treated and even the historic old Dinorwig slate quarry, which skirts the western foot of the mountain, is tidier and less gaunt than it was. To stand on the summit and to be told that beneath you are huge man-made caverns, housing an 1800-megawatt power plant takes some believing. There's no smoke, no fumes, no

Overleaf

ELECTRIC MOUNTAIN IN THE MAKING
Thousands of men and machines were used to construct this amazing power plant, but now it is finished and working there is, at all levels, a minimum labour force. With the upper level control room operating and monitoring through remote control, these machine-filled caverns create an eerie atmosphere of desertion.
Oil on canvas, 30"×40"

chimneys. Travel around to the other side of the upper mountain and you *do* come across something man-made, something that looks like a huge concrete wash basin, save that the plug hole is very big and obviously goes down a long way. Opinions differ: perhaps some think it's cosmetic treatment for an extinct volcano? Whatever it is it's about the only evidence to suggest that man might once more have mucked about with nature. In fact it is a safety valve. With millions of gallons of water being pumped around inside the mountain there has to be an outlet in the event of an unexpected surge of water pressure, whether from natural or unnatural sources.

Standing up here on some of the highest, greenest grass in Wales and smelling clean, unsullied wind from the sea it's not that easy to understand all this talk of some sort of Pied Piper's cave; so join me down below at the official entrance to the inside of Dinorwig's Electric Mountain. Here you will see how the waters from the upper lake Marchlyn Mawr (these magical Celtic names!) – 1500 million gallons in one cycle – are drawn through a series of tunnels finally to cascade down a spiral, vertical shaft to drive turbine blades which in turn drive the shaft to the generator. Don't ask me exactly how, but take it from the experts that somehow that deluge is so controlled that the final drive to the generator is maintained at 500 rpm – exactly synchronised with the National Grid frequency.

After leaving here, having contributed some 1800 megawatts to the national need, the waters are piped away to join the lower lake, Llyn Peris. Then, through the night, using National Grid power at its cheapest time, the turbines are reversed and the water is drawn back from Llyn Peris, pumped 476 yards up to the top of the mountain and piped back into Marchlyn Mawr to await day time and the next stopgap need.

Well, Newton proved the theory of gravity, but I bet he never thought of throwing the apples back up into the tree!

Figures on their own can become meaningless, but 3 million tonnes becomes a figure the mind can encompass when you enter the main machine hall. This was the amount of rock and spoil dug out during the construction of the underground site. Seeing the immense cavern of the central workings, big enough to hide a cathedral in, makes that figure totally believable. But *3 million tonnes* – where did it all go? The answer is, to the lower lake. To take it all, Llyn Peris had to be enlarged. Some of the surplus was used to create a new bed for that and the rest filled up the holes and scars left by the old slate quarry.

The next cavern is the transformer hall. It is noticeably lesser in size in only one respect – its interior height is a mere 60 feet here compared to some 200 feet in the main machine hall. Various interconnecting tunnels or galleries – busbar galleries, heating, ventilation and others – form a complex maze of underground workings extending to a total of some 10 miles. Not a place in which to go idly wandering!

Visually, Electric Mountain is tremendously impressive, but unless one worked there through its five-year gestation – two years digging the hole, three years building the plant – one can't comprehend a fraction of the overall achievement. So it *did* cost £450 million (which will be recouped over its first eight years' use),

The turbine hall, Electric Mountain
Watercolour, 22" × 15"

but recent history has seen equal if not greater sums of money written off on engineering or restructuring concepts which failed. Here thirty-six British engineering companies, small and large, combined to produce the largest pumped storage scheme in Europe and they all got it right first time.

The complex comprises 10 miles of tunnels and shafts (half of which are lined with concrete), a 650-yard rock-filled dam to enlarge Lake Marchlyn Mawr, and 400,000 cubic metres of concrete. There are as well six pump turbine plants, each producing 300 million watts, which are pushing the power through to six generator transformer units with the final output going through twin 400-kilovolt cables to the National Grid outside. Yet *all* this goes into an underground tunnel – no scenery-destroying overhead pylons with this scheme.

Dinorwig have published their own information leaflet giving all the facts and data, and it's an educational read indeed. They are justifiably proud of the conservation element, and the lengths to which they went to ensure that the salmon and trout population did not suffer from the marine intrusions are heartwarming. But when its achievements are summed up and boggled at, whether it is one of the best of its kind in Europe (or even in the world) or it can race from 0 to 1300 megawatts in less than 10 seconds – all this, for me, fades from my mind when I think of one man, perhaps the greatest engineer ever: Isambard Kingdom Brunel. Modern technicians may snort when I use I.K.B. as some sort of yardstick, but he would have approved of Electric Mountain. He was the only man who might have made it happen sooner. He was a man of infinite enterprise – resourceful enterprise – and Dinorwig is all of that.

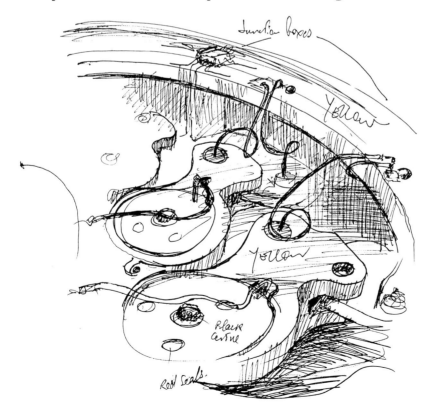

Control units at base of turbine shaft.

The Best Car in the World

ROLLS-ROYCE MOTOR CARS

*I*f it had been Smith & Jones, Hargreaves & Simpson, Cox & Matthews, it just wouldn't – *couldn't* – have been the same. But it so happened that it was the Hon. Charles Rolls who met up with Mr Henry Royce and ever since the alliterative and harmonious pairing of the two surnames has become synonymous with the finest four-wheeled product in the world. Possession of 'a Roller', as it is called in the slick *patois* of the City today, signifies not so much oneupmanship as arrivalship; the slightly older and more urbane speak of the 'Rolls'. It is less casual, a cultured name, but both of them immediately identify the Rolls-Royce.

As a car it does not compete with the Mercedes or keep ahead technically of the BMW; it simply continues to maintain a standard that has no counterpart, no comparison, anywhere in the world of motoring. There are faster cars, there are more powerful cars – just – and there are one or two bigger motors; nowhere else though is a car produced with such attention to detail. Nowhere else is there a car that from the bare bodyshell up has every component fitted by individual practised hand and checked by judgement of experienced eye.

It was not until I visited their production car factory at Crewe that I fully appreciated the statement 'The best car in the world'. Not until then did I realise that the Rolls-Royce workers look upon that most exalted sales slogan not as a proud, provocative challenge but as a simple statement of fact. As I toured the various shop floors, chatted to the workers, listened to the old-timers and watched steady, expert hands shaping, dressing and fitting metal, leather and wood with a patience and care that one rarely sees outside the nursing profession, one outstanding fact became obvious when I first asked the question: 'Proud of it? Our product? What we are doing? Oh, of course, you're bound to be proud of helping to build the best car in the world'. Foolish question, Maile. Young Paul, of whom I first asked this – to them – surprising and needless question, worked in the radiator shop. On that particular floor one man builds one radiator in approximately six hours; in that same time the more mundane motor manufacturer sees twenty or thirty finished cars pass along an assembly line controlled by computers and fed by robots.

Paul's radiator, in embryo form, was carried to his workbench. By him he has a drawer full of files, a bodyworker's hammer, an

engineer's steel rule, a vice and – most importantly – a soldering iron. No, not one of those modern electric jobs, but the old-fashioned sort, heavy, copper-headed and heated by a small brick-enclosed gas jet. A Rolls-Royce radiator (cost, about £1500) is the symbol of perfect precision, and yet the radiator is itself an illusion. What! Are we being hoodwinked? Yes, with the best of intentions: a perfectly flat and rectilinear surface, highly polished, through refracted light actually appears dished to the eye. So, the shells are cunningly made with subtle curves and ellipses to defeat the light and appear perfectly flat and in line. It's one of the few things that Royce can't take full credit for – Kallikrates designed the Parthenon using the same principles. Whether or not young Paul was aware of emulating a 5000-year-old design ploy I didn't find out, but I did discover that he is not averse to examining the more recent marques of Rolls-Royce that happen to be parked near wherever he may be. Simply the eye of the interested professional on his product, you would say, but, in Paul's case, there is a more significant reason: he can tell whether or not it's one of 'his' radiators and, if not, can possibly identify the craft of one in particular of his workmates. Now, if the Rolls-Royce owner stripped his car down and took off the radiator shell he would find initials stamped underneath and inside, and the 'history' book at Crewe would have recorded whose initials they were. But Paul and his mates, long after they have stamped their final seal on their handiwork, can identify from the outside

SILVER PLATED ROLLS-ROYCE SILVER GHOST
This beautiful machine has all the haughty grandeur that one expects of such a famous marque. I was permitted to sit in the driving seat and there fantasised that I was driving the car on its historic record-breaking run in 1907 from London to Edinburgh.
Acrylic and wash colour, 15" × 22"

form the fine, subtle variations of technique that separate one craftsman from another.

As every different craftsman's name who helped build each car is entered in the 'history' book that Rolls-Royce keep, I wouldn't have been surprised to learn that the upholsterer could also identify his seating finish, or the instrument panel fitter recognise his beautiful walnut veneer. When you follow a car's seemingly leisurely progress through its various stages of production, having infinite care and attention lavished upon it at every one, then you are prepared to believe almost anything of such a product. The matter of pride came up again when I met Jack Wheatley. Jack had worked for Rolls-Royce for forty-two years and now, impatient with retirement, spends much of his time acting as official guide for visitors to the works that he knows so well. Jack privately thought that some of the younger workers at Crewe did not serve quite the same disciplined apprenticeship as in his day. Here was perhaps the inevitable suspicion of the old towards the young, but he hammered at me with positive assertion. 'There's not one of 'em, man nor boy, who isn't as proud as punch working for Rolls-Royce. Aye', he said, as if reflecting on his earlier dubious view of youth, 'I'll give 'em that. They are proud all right of being Rolls-Royce – and so they should be'.

Rolls-Royce at Crewe began because of World War II. There was need for another 'shadow' factory to produce the famous Rolls-Royce Merlin aero engine. This was the engine that powered the Hurricanes and Spitfires in the Battle of Britain and later the Lancaster bomber, which I had myself flown in as a young airman. It was one of the wartime chapters that coloured many lives and events and would seem to have little to do with the Silver Spur and the Corniche motors of today. But this was the beginning of Rolls-Royce of Crewe and Jack had some very good tales to tell. He told of what was probably the one and only strike in the company's history.

The men had barely been in the newly built factory a year when the Ministry of Labour drafted in women to help produce the machines of war. The men were scandalised, or at the very least affronted; they didn't need women to help them build the phenomenal Merlin engine. (This was nearly fifty years ago, remember, and despite the ingress of the female into their territory during the previous conflict it was still very much a man's world). So they struck – for one week. I never did discover from Jack whether it was intended to be no more than just a token strike or whether after that time they realised the despised intruders were doing a capable job. 'Twelve women they brought in, and we went on strike', twinkled Jack. 'A fortnight later we had 300 women working alongside us!' When pressed he said, still smiling at old memories, 'Oh it wasn't so bad – the things that went on in between putting Merlins together...' There obviously had been no need for another strike!

The future of Rolls-Royce cars received a shock wave on 29 December 1940, when a lone German Heinkel bombed the factory. That Luftwaffe pilot wasn't concerned with the Camargues and Corniches to come forty years later, he just wanted to make a severe dent in the production line of Hitler's most hated internal

combustion engine. But he created only a very small dent. The factory continued and by 1945 Jack and his fellow workers had produced 26,000 Rolls-Royce aero engines, all used in the war.

In that same year Crewe converted to the production of Rolls-Royce motor cars. Derby, having also been engaged on aero engine production, decided they would stay with that up-and-coming industry, and leave the less technologically exciting car division at Crewe. Less exciting maybe, but as Rolls-Royce Ltd Aero Engine Division progressed into the ever expanding world of aero engine development, requiring massively increased finance to keep pace with increasing research programmes, the traditional world of Silver Wraiths and Bentleys at Crewe continued, steadily producing some forty or fifty cars a week and selling every one. The Aero Engine Division, pressured by government, economic forces and foreign competition, found themselves in a financial quagmire where never-ending research and development costs had outstripped all capital investment potential. Unfortunately, Crewe and Derby were one and the same company, and in 1971 the world famous car company was forced to accept the humiliation of receivership alongside its much larger aero engine division.

Electing to cater for the new breed of wide-bodied jets being introduced by America, Rolls-Royce had come up with the RB211. Constantly changing and critical demands from the Lockheed

1907 Silver Ghost at 1986 Veteran Car Rally, Hyde Park.
Wash colour, study for oil, 15"×22"

ENGINE ASSEMBLY LINE AT
CREWE
I watched the finest engine in the
world being produced. The major
tools in use were the oldest tools
given to man – hands, eyes and ears.
There is little outward sign of
twentieth-century automation and
robot-controlled mass production.
Such is their application and attention
to detail that one sees these workers
as craftsmen rather than engineers.
Watercolour and acrylic, 17"×25"

Aircraft Company sent the aero division on a punitive course of
never-ending development research. It was a non-productive
programme that was meat and drink to the engineer but a
nightmare for the accountants and, whilst they forced the
engineers eventually to swallow the bitter truth at Derby, there
could be no reconciliation with the facts for the workforce of the
Motor Car Division at Crewe.

On 4 February of that year the truth, in the guise of a wild early
morning rumour, was horribly confirmed by David Plastow,
managing director, when he called the employees together for an
'important announcement'. As a stunned workforce listened to his
sombre words, they knew why truckloads of materials had been
halted at the gates that morning. Those same supplies were now
being sent back on their return journey. 'That really brought it
home to us', said one employee, remembering. Others
unashamedly admitted to silent, emotional tears and a suggestion
at the time that they would work weekends without pay to keep the
company going was supported unanimously. But it would have
taken a thousand weekends of Silver Shadow production to make
an appreciable dent in the massive debt incurred by their partner
division and time had run out; there were no weekends in the credit
column. It was the end – or should have been.

Royce the engineer might have sympathised with the Derby

engineers' fruitless pursuit of excellence. Rolls, the entrepreneur salesman, killed in typically adventurous circumstances*, would surely have supported Crewe loyalties. Perhaps the Official Receiver, Rupert Nicholson, arriving promptly at 10 o'clock that morning was sympathetic to the memory of both, or did he have secret loyalties himself? Whatever his brief, it is commendable that he wasted no time examining books and viability at Crewe; within twenty-four hours the workforce were back at their jobs, suppliers were alerted to return and the order books opened again.

It had all been nightmarish but, being Rolls-Royce, there was no grim period of entrenchment. Barely a fortnight later the motoring press, still speculating on the Silver Shadow's future, were beaten totally at their own game when Rolls-Royce grandly and blandly announced their new model, the Corniche. It was to be, and still is, the finest open tourer in the world. The moral is, if you are going to make a comeback then make it with style – and this was style that no-one could match.

---

*The Hon. Charles Rolls was the first Englishman to be killed in a powered flying accident, at Bournemouth on 12 July 1910.

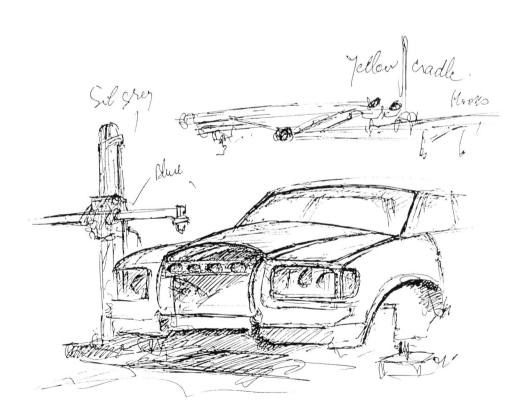

Defence of the Realm

I had marvelled at the superb Rolls-Royce engineering when studying the finest car in the world at Crewe, but hadn't anticipated seeing it (the engine, that is) again in such a totally different context. In aircraft building, yes, or possibly in some expensive marine role, but perhaps not quite such a long way from Crewe. Here I was up on Tyneside, looking at a massive, formidable army tank in the new, highly efficient Vickers Defence Systems factory. Forty tons of armoured weight and still able to travel at over 40 m.p.h., and there was the familiar Rolls-Royce valve cover topping the 800 h.p. engine.

Tyneside has seen industrial giants and industrial fortunes rise and fall over the years since the Industrial Revolution started it all. Only a few hundred yards up the river is the site of the old Elswick plant where the seeds of the great Vickers enterprise were first planted. Sir William Armstrong was another product of an age that saw such giants as Watt, Stephenson, Brunel and Telford hone their talents into historic achievements. Armstrong contributed equally as much to that era of industrial change and invention and not the least part of this was his radical development of hydraulics. But, rightly or wrongly, it was his involvement with the military gun that tends to single him out in history. He was the first Englishman to design and build a rifle-barrelled field gun, and also by force of character persuaded the stick-in-the-mud government ministers of the day to adopt it for the British Army.

But all that was in early Victorian times. Many partnerships and collaborations followed before the present-day company built their new factory along the Scotswood Road in Newcastle-on-Tyne to supply tanks and other tracked vehicles – all with rifle-barrelled guns – to armed forces across the entire world.

Back in the late nineteenth century the Vickers brothers were making the American Maxim gun under licence before they eventually produced their own famous Vickers machine gun. This gun, which helped the British Tommy win so many battles in World War I, was used in the Afghanistan frontier battles between the wars and was still a front line weapon in the opening days of World War II.

Vickers built the first British tank and, with just one exception, have designed and built every other since. One of their latest and most successful is the Mk3 battle tank. They seem to fight shy of names nowadays – since the Centurion, the Chieftain and the Challenger, new models are brusquely allocated mark numbers. If

they wanted, they could have given the Mk3 several names for Vickers designed this model to fulfill a variety of different roles.

If you want a 38-tonner that will travel over almost any terrain anywhere in the world, with a 105 mm gun fitted with laser sighting, at some 40 m.p.h. then the Mk3 fits the bill. You can check the secondary armourment, variously mounted 7.62 mm machine guns, when you order. You can also decide then whether you prefer the Rolls-Royce 800 h.p. four-stroke diesel or the General Motors 720 h.p. two-stroke. But if your army is concerned with retrieving and repairing other tanks and vehicles still on the battlefield then that army still needs the Mk3 battle tank, but this time it has become the ARRV (armoured repair and recovery vehicle – couldn't they just call it the Retriever?). Built on the same heavily armoured chassis, this is a comprehensively equipped travelling workshop and breakdown vehicle. Its winch/crane can straight pull or tow up to 25 tonnes, but with multi revving of its power plant it can pull up to 75 tonnes – useful when another tracked vehicle or carrier is bogged down. The crane can clean lift 4 tonnes.

There are rivers to cross? Two versions of the Mk3 (armoured bridgelayers) take care of this problem. There is a choice of the class 60 bridging system No.9, where the vehicle lowers the bridging section from the vertical – rather like the bascules of Tower Bridge. But the Vickers Mk3 takes these bascules anywhere across country

DRESSED FOR THE BATTLEFIELD
An army's role in conventional warfare still demands conventional weapons, but what a sophisticated conventional weapon this is. The Mk3 battle tank, with its mobility over the most hostile terrain, its 105mm gun, 7.62 mm and 12.7 mm machine guns and smoke dischargers, is a compact fighting force in its own right.
Wash and pen, 15"×22"

to span a 40-foot river. Or, if the river is wider you call up the horizontally launched Biber Bridge, which extends forward some 24 yards of metal roadway.

Then there's the air defence vehicle. Yes, it's still a battle tank Mk3 variety, fitted with twin, radar-controlled 35 mm ack-ack guns. But if you really want to bring in the heavy brigade then the VSPH (Vickers self-propelled howitzer) is the answer. A specially designed turret is fitted with a 155 mm howitzer — now *that* is heavy artillery in any army's ordnance book. Though the Mk3 and its variants are best-sellers Vickers do not rely upon that success. For the classical role of the heavy tank they have produced the Mk7 — 25 feet long, 55 tonnes battle weight, and with a 120 mm rifled gun as main armourment. All this is backed up by 7.62 mm m/g and grenade dischargers which fire either anti personnel or smoke grenades.

This monster with its 1500 h.p. engine can travel on the road at 50 m.p.h. If you were to stand beside its great bulk, so ponderous looking as the motor starts, it would seem easy to race away from it on foot. It's deceptive. Daley Thompson might beat it over the first hundred yards, lesser mortals would still need their litre or so of automatic power.

The range extends further to a 16-tonne infantry combat vehicle, another smaller (7 tonnes) wheeled vehicle, which Vickers *have* given a name to — the Fox — a fast (70 m.p.h.) lightweight, armoured car that can carry a variety of weapons, including a 30 mm cannon, and is a favourite with the army for parachute·drop exercises.

Ah yes, there is one other name — the Valkyr. This too is 'airportable'. A wheeled vehicle capable of 75 m.p.h. despite its weight of nearly 12 tonnes, it is also fully amphibious. The weight is due to its armoured protection, which is far superior to the plating normally given to armoured cars or personnel carriers. The Valkyr's protective cladding can withstand direct hits from armour-piercing 7.62 mm fire at point blank range and even against 155 mm shell splinters. Like the Mk3 battle tank it has a variety of roles: personnel carrier, fire support vehicle, and security vehicle. When this sort of multi-purpose vehicle is looked at together with its larger stablemate the Mk3 in all its different guises, one can understand why Vickers are winning such a sizeable chunk of the export market in the defence industry.

From Elswick to Scotswood Road

The new factory is notable for two factors. One is its size — or rather its length — for it is the longest single roof unit I have ever seen. The other factor is its simplicity, maximised by acres of vast floor space.

As the tank family developed and became more armoured and so much heavier, the conventional factory of the past became quite inadequate. When parts of a single product can be measured in tonnes rather than hundredweights and even a locking bolt weigh as much as a small car's back axle, the workforce doesn't want to be collecting each of these components from separate areas. The solution was delightfully simple: one immense long workshop with

Mk 7 battle tank
Wash and pen, 11" × 15"

plenty of floor space. The raw material or basic castings all come in at one end and as each stage is worked upon and assembled so it moves on, proceeding (in Vickers Defence Systems' case) from west to east until the final finished product is at the ready for delivery. I never saw the old Elswick factory, but judging from pictures it would seem to have been a typical Victorian or post-Victorian building. One imagines that function and economy had been the ruling specifications. When the Factory Act and various other pieces of industrial legislation made themselves felt there were, no doubt, additions and alterations, none of which could have helped its efficiency.

I talked to some of the workers who remembered Elswick well. Loyalty obviously influenced their views but their nostalgia was reserved for remembered comrades and comic incidents. The easy, light and spacious atmosphere surrounding them here at Scotswood Road needs no such sweeteners to win their approval.

The only thing this splendid new factory lacks, as yet, is history. Elswick naturally cornered the market in that product. Battleships for the Russo-Japanese war were built on its riverside yards. Hydraulic machinery and cranes for the new railways of the day were produced there, as was a railway bridge for the East India Company. It turned out underwater mines for the Crimean War and, of course, guns, among them the first 'rifled' breach-loading 12-pounder in the 1850s. And in 1870 Elswick built thirty-one, 100-tonne 18-inch guns for the Italian shore defence forces. They did not shy away from the challenge of size, those Victorians.

But it was a later historic piece of munitions making that took my interest. We all of us know something of the World War II raids on the Möhne Dam. The famous 'Dambuster' squadron and Barnes

Wallis have gone into the history books – but what about the bomb itself, the 'Bouncing Bomb' that breached the wall of the dam and brought the war a year nearer to its end? Yes: that was built at Elswick too.

Vickers products thus helped shorten World War II. Now they not only strengthen the defences of our realm but win us much needed export trade all over the world.

Tank production at the Scotswood factory
Watercolour and acrylic, 17" × 25"

To Penicillin – and Beyond

THE BEECHAM GROUP

One can play intriguing games with a little historical knowledge of a specific subject.

If we were to pose a quiz question such as 'What international company can be linked with a renowned cricketer, the Royal Air Force and a famous conductor?', it would probably fox more than a few. If, however, we add the word 'pharmaceutical', then on the strength of the famous conductor many would no doubt guess correctly at Beecham. But what of the cricketer and the RAF?

Well, Beecham now own Brylcreem and an older generation will well remember Denis Compton, possibly one of the first cult figures to be used for commercial advertising. And the RAF? Well, in the early days of World War II they were also known as the 'Brylcreem boys'. They suffered this slightly patronising title until they won their spurs. Beecham acquired the Brylcreem product in 1939 and their shrewd and profitable use of (for those days) such penetrating advertising would have earned the approval of their founder, the first Thomas Beecham.

Born in the little Oxfordshire village of Curbridge in 1820, Thomas was the eldest of a farm labourer's seven children. He spent one year at the village school, probably one of the 'penny schools' of the day; then, at the age of eight, began work as a shepherd boy. According to his biography, it was now that he began to study the medicinal properties of herbs. It is hard to believe that at eight or nine years old young Beecham studied, analysed and applied the principles of herbal cures, but certainly, somewhere along that farm labourer's, or perhaps his mother's, bloodline had passed not only a bright intelligence but an industrious and enterprising character. Before he was twenty Beecham was making herbal remedies for both human and animal use, selling them at the country markets and fairs which then were the rural communities' major shopping centres. Looking for a wider market, he heard of the expanding population 'up north' where the Industrial Revolution was making its first impact, and in 1847 he moved to Lancashire. By 1850 he had acquired a licence to sell medicines and set up trade in Wigan as 'Thomas Beecham, Chemist, Druggist and Tea Dealer'. We may think that the mail order business is one of the inventions of the twentieth century, but two hundred years ago it was the method by which probably some 50 per cent of the populace did a large, or at least the specialised, part of their shopping.

With railways still in their infancy and road travel only for tinkers, the adventurous and the wealthy, city shopping had a limited custom. Rural England wanted and needed the services of those traders and the businessmen who offered their services and their products through the pages of the respectable county press. In 1859 the first Beecham advertisement appeared. Beecham's curative products (sales of groceries and tea helped pay the rent) numbered only four in those days: a pill with the euphemistic title of 'Female's Friend', a 'Royal Toothpowder', a 'Golden Tooth Tincture' and – the one that was to win world fame – 'Beecham's Pills'.

In an age where organic illness was usually met with either leeching or purging, Beecham's Pills were the product that laid the foundation of future success. Without doubt Thomas's very real skills as a herbalist triumphed in a market where quacks and charlatans proliferated. It was not unknown for some of the advertised products 'guaranteed to cure all ills' even to have a modicum of salt petre if not actual dynamite in their preparation. How the sufferers must thankfully have subscribed to Beecham's Pills!

That same year Thomas Beecham closed his shop in Wigan and moved to another industrial town not far away, St Helens. It was here that the shepherd-cum-herbalist showed his business flair and set up mechanised production of his products. By 1887 his queue of customers stretched as far as Africa and Australia and that first small factory was insufficient to cope with demand. His son Joseph helped set up the new factory and with the progress of time gradually took over more of the running of the business.

Joseph was as go-ahead as his father and introduced the famous pills to the United States in 1888 (with an added sweetener to please American palates) and he continued as well to extend their advertising. Towards the end of the nineteenth century 14,000 newspapers worldwide regularly carried Beecham advertisements. In 1895 Thomas Beecham formally retired but still kept an active interest in the business up to his death in 1907. His skills as a herbalist must surely have contributed to his own good health, for he reached the age of eighty seven at a time when curative medicine and surgery was still a long way from the wonder drugs and techniques of more recent years.

Expansion continued to be the order of the day until 1916, when Joseph died. The company's success had brought to the lowly shepherd's son a knighthood, then a baronetcy. Such wealth and success was in an oblique way to cause a marking time in the affairs of the great company. With such social standing in the family children followed appropriate social patterns and turned to culture and the arts. Grandson of the founder, the second Thomas took to music. The factory at St Helens producing a million of the famous pills a day held no attractions for him – which was just as well, otherwise the music world would have been the poorer for the loss of a brilliant conductor. But with him he took the last of the Beecham drive and flair. The executors who ran the company after Joseph's death were efficient, but no more, and but for the arrival on the scene of one Phillip Hill, in 1924, who knows whether or not the company might have become quite moribund.

The Beecham estate, apart from its commercial viability, had assets, the prize of which was the freehold of Covent Garden Market and the famous Opera House. Although such a valuable property must have been the plum that attracted Phillip Hill he soon recognised the potential of the pill business. He initiated a period of expansion and development built upon acquisition, a concept new to business in those days but one which has stayed with Beecham's ever since.

In 1928 Beecham's Pills became a public company and the various acquisitions or controlling interests in such firms as Veno's, Yeast-Vite, Iron Jelloids, Phosferine and Phyllosan followed. The growing market in ladies' beauty products took them into toiletries when they bought out the producers of the famous Amami shampoos. Since the days of their founder, though, they had not really returned to herbal or chemical research back at the laboratory. Their continuing acquisitions policy seemed to be taking them ever further away from original productive pharmaceutical work. Other famous marketing products that fell to Beecham bids were Eno's Fruit Salts and, as we mentioned earlier, in 1939 Brylcreem. Ownership of such companies tied up massive capital and there seems to have been neither the wish nor the money available for expensive chemical research and developments. In 1938, however, the acquisition of Macleans for the princely sum of £2,300,000 was quickly followed by the purchase of Lucozade, which was to prove a tremendous profit earner. In 1953 it accounted for 50 per cent of Beecham's total profit, so more capital became available. But what Macleans also brought into the fold was a director called H. G. Lazell. Remember back in the 1850s the 'Royal Toothpowder' and the 'Golden Tooth Tincture' that Thomas Beecham purveyed? Strange that a toothpaste company should act as a catalyst for later fortunes.

It was Lazell, always a firm believer in scientific research, who, in 1943, chose the right moment to persuade the whole board to adopt a new philosophy. A cleverly orchestrated appeal for the formation of 'Beecham Research Laboratories' met with total success and a team of 115 laboratory workers headed by 34 graduate scientists was appointed with laboratories at Macleans's headquarters at Brentford (now the Beecham Group head-quarters).

In 1945 Brockham Park, a country house 25 miles away in Surrey, was selected as a permanent headquarters for the research and development team. When in 1949 Beecham bought its first prescriptive medical company they were able to centralise research at Brockham Park, basically keeping to pharmaceutical work. Their new company, C. L. Bencard, was small, but for the first time gave them their entry into the true medical market. Bencard, specialists in allergy vaccines, had productive expertise and marketing knowledge in an area totally new to Beecham, and this was to open up a new world to the company.

It was Lazell who transformed Beecham from a medium size company into an international force. Acquisitions still continued. During the fifties and sixties came Ribena, PLJ, Horlicks. Bovril followed in 1980 and many other well known names in the toiletries field came under the company's wing. But the real star in the group

BROCKHAM PARK
This dignified and elegant country house provided the laboratory for the famous breakthrough in penicillin research in 1957.
Watercolour, 17" × 25"

arose as a result of Bencard's capabilities and Lazell's planning.

Penicillin, to begin with the miracle healer, had become by the fifties a medical problem. Its use, so abundant and widespread, gave the germs it had originally defeated the chance to fight back. Enzyme-producing bacteria was now actually destroying the penicillin. To appreciate, even remotely, subsequent achievements of Beecham's scientists, we have to be aware of some of the molecular structures involved here. Penicillin's structure is such that it has a 'tail' or chain of atoms which controls its therapeutic character. Therefore this 'tail' is what had to be concentrated upon to restore to penicillin its original powers as a wonder drug. Medical laboratories across the world were working on the problem, many of them pursuing the same course as Beecham, ie. to produce a penicillin with a different 'tail' – in other words a chemically manipulated drug. But while this work was going on, in 1957, different though parallel experimental research made Beecham's Brockham Park laboratories world famous. Talk to any research chemist of '6–APA' and he will nod knowingly 'Brockham Park, the big penicillin breakthrough in 1957'. And 6-APA? Let us not get too immersed in science again: sufficient to say that the boffins at Brockham Park discovered a penicillin nucleus, without a tail or side chain, called '6-amino penicillanic acid', hence 6–APA. All they needed to do now was to produce it in quantity – and produce as well a quantity of synthetic side chains which could contain the necessary properties to combat a known range of bacteria and join one to the other. That is really an over-simplification of what science can achieve with intense, detailed and dedicated laboratory research. That a new factory was built at Worthing for the sole purpose of producing it is a measure of how important a task it was.

That particular breakthrough was one of the historic highlights of antibiotics research which is still going on but now there is also considerable work going on into the cause and remedy of cardio-vascular disease. With Beecham's experience in pharmaceutical research they are well placed to find answers to this particular twentieth-century affliction.

Today, Beecham's assets are still strong in consumer products, be it Bovril, a glass of fruit juice or toothpaste. They also have twenty-seven pharmaceutical factories around the world and were one of the first boldly to enter the tough United States market and acquire existing successful American companies, both pharmaceutical and consumer.

One hundred and forty years ago a young shepherd boy discovered the curative properties of dandelions, fennel and elecampane. When he proudly set up his market stall in Wigan, officially licensed to sell his herbal medicines, did he ever dream of how one day those small beginnings might develop?

Technicians check fermentation plant.

Dounreay – The Nuclear Future

UK ATOMIC ENERGY AUTHORITY

This comment is not intended to provoke CND enthusiasts but it would, without doubt, be very difficult to organise an effective demonstration against this particular atomic power station. For a start, few, if any adherents to such a protest could be raised from the local populace. Indeed it's unlikely that any such organisers combing the whole of Caithness would have much success. It would have to be either a press gang or their modern equivalent, 'flying pickets'. I base such a declaration on happenings in 1954, all set in train by one person, that person being Lord Hinton.

Lord Hinton, that remarkable character who virtually masterminded Dounreay, acted then in a manner quite out of character, out of character that is with the persona he outwardly appeared to represent. Hinton was after all primarily a scientist. He also carried considerable clout with his ministerial contacts. Furthermore, he was something of a visionary and visionaries are not swayed by current social views.

Some years earlier, Hinton, with a small team of researchers, including Dounreay's former director Cliff Blumfield, had convinced the government that atomic energy was the viable alternative to coal, gas and oil. In the fifties, Britain's power demands were constantly increasing, threatening to outstrip supply (North Sea oil had not been dreamed of). They produced a paper of sufficient strength to win them ministerial backing and – more importantly – money. It was enough to have tempted many men in recent times to march into whatever tract of countryside they required and exercise their prerogative first, leaving questions and objections for later. They might well have employed the *fait accompli* tactic, used so often by those in authority this century. Hinton, however, did none of that. He went first with a handful of specialists up north to Dounreay, more specifically to the little town of Thurso, whose inhabitants would be the most affected by such a questionable, industrial imposition. They held a series of meetings with the canny Scots of northern Caithness. Nothing was concealed. Probably, for the first time in history, a whole town was given a comprehensive science lesson in nuclear fission. All plans of the proposed Dounreay unit, which was, in effect, to be a full-scale experimental model fast atomic reactor, were put on display for all to see and to question. The people of Thurso and the farmers and the crofters from around looked and listened. They questioned Hinton's team

Service replacement on the reactor floor at Dounreay.
Watercolour, 22" × 15"

and they got truthful answers. All possible hazards were explained and so, of course, were the benefits.

Consequently, the first successful fast atomic reactor in Europe was built. Without appeals, demonstrations or objections, it was built in record time (such a feat would be impossible today). It opened in 1959 to produce subsequently its forecast 15 MW of electric power. Enough power to supply a town of fifteen thousand people. It closed down in 1977 when its successor Prototype Fast Reactor reached full thermal power. All the possible hazards are contained in leadlined, one yard thick concrete inner walls, a constantly duplicated system of electronic and manual safety checks, and a safety design brief that has formed the basis for all atomic power stations since built in western Europe. The benefits were clear from the very start, all of them centering obviously on the one prime factor: employment.

Dounreay itself now employs over 2,000 people, and the indirect benefits are self-evident when you visit the area. Thurso itself has expanded from a population of barely three thousand to near ten thousand. Material reason enough you might say for people in a once severely depressed area to stifle any fears and suspicions they might hold towards such a benefactor. But remember, these people *know*. They know the radiation capability of the canisters of uranium regularly trucked into the plant to feed the furnace (that, very simply is what an atomic reactor is). They know what radiation levels may exist around any job they take on in Dounreay itself. Husbands and wives, brothers, sons and sisters of Thurso are all part of Dounreay. Some are canteen workers, cleaners, drivers, others are electricians, engineers, technicians. They range from school leavers through a floating working population to university graduates. They all make up the hi-tech, twenty-first-century complex of Dounreay. All of them from time to time receive the sort of medical checkups that can only be associated with the chemistry that gave the world The Bomb. Those in certain designated areas carry their own personal gamma-sensitive film badge* and monitor their own radiation levels, seriously and responsibly, but not, I would add, with any undue tension. To its human neighbours Dounreay has displaced bleak Social Security. It hasn't created any millionaires, or even wealth, but it has given a degree of stability and security to an area that was dying. Instead of people constantly leaving, the migration pattern has reversed and what was once an area of great natural beauty – able only to support a handful of crofters, a small fishing fleet and tiny moribund township – now not only still has its natural beauty, a high level of permanent employment and a town that has steadily grown away from its geriatric tendencies.

From neither neighbours nor employees is there any suggestion of stoic resignation. From the hospitable, middle-aged lady behind the bar (Caithness doesn't seem to produce the orthodox barmaid) came a very matter of fact comment: 'Och. It's been a boon tae us. Back before all the young laddies would be awae heading south. We were dying – now we are living agin.'

*A dosimeter.

In the plant itself there are jobs, *good* jobs, and good pay from a good employer with good working conditions. For those closer to the actual production side, appreciation of those facts is complemented by pride, warm pride that is often expressed in a flippant, jocular affection. A relief shift on the PFR (prototype fast reactor) floor is greeted with: 'The old girl is going well today, don't upset her' – the same sort of shared affection that sailors feel towards their ship.

Like any other power station, Dounreay produces steam to turn the turbines that finally produce the megawatts. If there has been a 'shut down' for maintenance, the steam workers jibe the PFR side, 'Come on we're all ready and waiting – get her cooking', and if one of the turbines should suffer some ailment then the electrical technicians get flak from both sides. 'Hey, the old girl's cooking up a fine head of steam and you're letting it go to waste! Get your finger out!'

I stood, quite safely, on the lid of 'the old girl' when I visited, seemingly greatly daring, but there would have been more action – and danger – on the footplate of a high-speed locomotive. There was a constant background hum of generator noise re-echoing back through metal girders and pipework, but one needed reminding that there were 600 million watts of thermal heat being generated 50 feet below, as well as the clinical orderliness around the working area above. The 'steam room' and the turbine hall gave a greater impression of power. There the noise was quite deafening. With the tremendous concrete walls, impregnated with lead, the noise could not escape, so in these sections ear protectors as well as your hard hat were essential.

One could get accustomed to the 'check gates', facsimiles of the security detectors at Heathrow, except that these were checking for the minutest rise in body radioactivity. Everybody entering and leaving the reactor floor has to pass through them at various intervals. What a layman finds – and this emphasises the James Bond element of Dounreay – is the series of airlocks one has to pass through on entering and leaving the PFR. Those massive alarmed and wheel–locked doors, that can never be opened together, take one beyond 007 to *Startrek*. Their purpose is to maintain controlled air pressures and lower inside pressure and higher outside ensure that any possible leaks do not immediately become fugitive. The unequal pressures keep them inside where they can be dealt with. So very simple, but so very effective.

Such detailed, meticulous precautions somehow complement the thoughtful preparations made by Hinton thirty years ago at the beginning of the story.

Dounreay: the first prototype fast
reactor.
Acrylic and oil, 30" × 40"

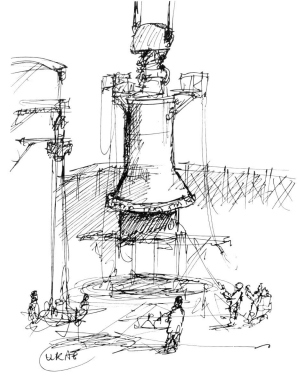

A Nobel Enterprise

IMPERIAL CHEMICAL INDUSTRIES

The first British manufacturing company to reach a £1 billion per year (pretax) profit, ICI is the world's fifth largest chemical company.

Such a company, producing goods in forty overseas countries as well as in the UK, having 14,000 different products, holding 150,000 patents on new inventions or product names, and able to spend more than a million pounds a day on research, must obviously have quite a history behind it. It has, but not all that long a history – at least not as Imperial Chemical Industries. Significant leads up to its birth can be traced back a little over a hundred years. In the little town of Helensborg, Sweden, a ramshackle wooden workshop was blown skyhigh with its five occupants. The shocking tragedy may not have surprised some of the locals who were wary of that scientist mucking about with nitro glycerine. That episode started a train of events that would do justice to a Hollywood soap epic. The rich tapestry of this company history is certainly well embroidered. What with leading politicians, famous arms dealers, a post-World War I industrial espionage excursion that reads like a Frederick Forsyth novel, transatlantic dashes in the great liners of the age, and the joint suicide of a leading industrialist and his wife, there is certainly more drama packed into ICI's beginnings than we could possibly relate here. Sadly we have to just skate over the surface of it now. (For a full and enthralling account, read Caroline Kennedy's *'ICI, The Company That Changed Our Lives'*).

The blowing up of that wooden workshop in Sweden would seem to be the classic fate of a mad scientist at work – but the scientist wasn't mad at all and, tragically and yet fortunately, it wasn't the scientist of historic significance who died in that experiment but his brother. The one who lived and was to make the name so famous carried on with his experiments that eventually gave the world dynamite. Immanuel Nobel *did* produce a relatively safe and stable plastic explosive.

So it was the inventors of dynamite, Immanuel and Alfred Nobel, who were the founders of ICI? No, not exactly, but they must be mentioned, however briefly, as important figures in ICI's early years. By 1868 the demand for the new wonder explosive was such that an international network of companies was set up to produce dynamite. Immanuel and son Alfred were honoured with Sweden's premier award, the Gold Medal of the Swedish Academy of Sciences. While the Nobels were raising big bangs all around the world, another scientist, not quite so spectacularly but nonetheless

THE *AQUITANIA*
Where ICI was born. The *Aquitania*
left New York on 6 October 1926 with
the dynamic McGowan on board with
the Brunner, Mond party. Its six-day
voyage was remarkable only for the
business agreement reached that was
to have a great and far reaching
influence on the whole chemical
industry.

The 'Aquitania Agreement' as it
became known, typed out on the
ship's Cunard Line paper, formed the
basis for the creation of the great
company ICI.
Watercolour, 15" × 22"

as surely, was developing a process for producing soda ash. This in
turn led to the scientist, Ludwig Mond, forming a partnership with
John Tomlinson Brunner from Cheshire and becoming a leading
alkali manufacturer.

Mond could well be labelled the earliest industrial
conservationist. His activities in this field may not much resemble
the modern ethos of conservation, but he certainly abhorred waste
and it was his research into the saving of waste in industry and the
recycling of waste materials which in the late nineteenth century
must have made at least a small hole in the black front of
atmospheric and terrestrial pollution that descended with the
Industrial Revolution.

There were many trials and tribulations in the careers of both
Brunner, Mond and the Nobel company before they became,
respectively, the world's biggest alkali manufacturing company and
a powerful international explosives company. War often creates
unusual partnerships. That Brunner, Mond and the Nobels should
find some common ground for business association is not
surprising, but a layman might wonder why the British dye
industry features in this strange chemical history. Well, Brunner,
Mond and Nobel Industries were close enough in a lot of research
fields and when ammonium nitrate was needed to fill the demand

for amatol (another propellant explosive) Brunner, Mond were asked to supply the ammonium nitrate, which brought the two companies closer still. In addition to the weapons of the First World War, literally millions of khaki uniforms were needed for the British Tommies. One of the basic compounds in the dyes used for the fabric of those uniforms was coal tar, which was also used in the production of TNT. So, those two contradictory wartime demands strengthened and enriched all those companies.

That a modern historian should refer to Alfred Nobel as one of 'ICI's godfathers' was perhaps an unconscious irony. Some of his successors in the business world of the twenties and thirties may not exactly have been *mafiosi* but they were no slouches in the cut and thrust of the international business world. By the mid twenties, notwithstanding having to relinquish their nitrogen fixing process to the British, the parent company of BASF – IG Farben – had once more become an all-powerful industrial company. Brunner, Mond and Nobel Industries, equally powerful in the UK, operated satisfactory cartel agreements with the Germans that kept everyone happy – until, that is, the Americans came over again, or threatened to. Orlando F. Weber, whose propensity for instant sackings earned him the sobriquet of 'the Fire Chief' was determined to make his already big Allied Chemical & Dye Corporation even bigger. With assets of nearly £300 million behind them, AC & DC were a formidable force and their threat of invading the European market was alarming. Not only would the Europeans' comfortably agreed export trades be knocked for six, their own home markets would come under fire too.

Nobel Industries did what those under threat had done before them from time immemorial, they went into the enemy camp. Approaches were made to Allied's biggest USA competitors, DuPont de Nemours of Delaware, and the plot really began to thicken. DuPont had substantial shares in General Motors. Nobel had been actively considering the production of motor car components (fabrics and cellulose) so there was a double interest. DuPont also had agreements with British Dyestuffs, and it was in the dye industry that the German IG Farben held the biggest advantage over the British chemical industry. The possibility of increasing the strength of their own dyestuffs with this enforced approach to the Americans was an added attraction.

There now followed, from January to September 1926, a series of meetings that involved Sir Harry McGowan, chairman of Nobel's, Roscoe Brunner and Sir Alfred Mond, an ex-Chancellor of the Exchequer, Solvay's of Belgium, Allied Industries, DuPont's, IG Farben and Lord Ashfield (British Dyestuffs) to name the principal participants. The purposes of the meetings were, variously, to form an amalgamation of British companies spoken of as a 'British IG', an affiliation of DuPont, IG Farben and Allied Industries, and a merger of Brunner, Mond and Nobel Industries – and that is quoting only those agendas which seem to have been recorded. Initially, with two such opposite characters as McGowan and Mond any get together between their two companies looked doomed to failure. It seemed natural that Alfred Mond would lean more to some form of German alliance.

MERSEYSIDE IN THE 1880s
This was a common scene on the Mersey, in the Midlands and in parts of the North East through the years of the Industrial Revolution. Vast quantities of hydrochloric acid and sulphuric acid belched into the upper atmosphere to return eventually to earth as acid rain. Ludwig Mond, with his hatred of waste in the chemical industry, was one of the earliest of conservationists. His process for recovering sulphur from alkali waste was to effect an economic new system of producing soda, a key chemical in many industries. Mond's process reduced the hydrochloric acid in chimney flues and also reduced the many rotting dumps of sulphur/alkali waste that littered the countryside.

A final scheme that excluded Nobel's was based on the success of IG Farben's radical oil from coal process – a process as attractive to the Americans as to the British – and if agreed would have given the Germans an incredible controlling interest in the world's chemical industry. McGowan, his combative Glaswegian instincts surfacing strongly at being left out of that particular meeting, had his own plans. As a director of British Dyestuffs he immediately opposed Lord Ashfield's part in the proposed alliance and the rest of the board were still getting over the shock of his broadside to them when he boarded the *Mauretania* at Southampton. The liner was the right vessel for such a character as McGowan: Blue Riband record holder, she left on 18 September and arrived at New York six days later. Talks between Allied Industries, Solvay, Brunner, Mond and IG were well under way when McGowan arrived. The Nobel man brooked no ceremony, virtually demanding that the British companies should form their own merger. Together, he argued, they had the strength to resist the American invasion and to compete as they always had done with the Germans, but now from greater strength. There was just the slight threat too of Nobel's going it alone to join IG Farben, but it was probably not needed. McGowan was a powerful persuader.

Another great liner, the *Aquitania*, took McGowan and the Brunner Mond party back to England. Somewhere on that lavishly luxurious voyage ICI was born. The British amalgamation consisted of Nobel's, Brunner, Mond, British Dyestuffs and United

Alkali. British Dyestuffs needed strengthening, and willy-nilly had to agree whether they approved of McGowan's cavalier tactics or not. At the time United Alkali did not even know the deed was done and again it took the Nobel chairman's persuasive powers for them to agree the plans.

Empire trading had always been one of the prerogatives of both companies (the red colouring on the world map of those days indicated the vast amount of worldwide markets this afforded) and the intention to further this was shown in the choice of Imperial Chemical Industries for a title. ICI effectively began operating in January 1927 with 33,000 employees. Those employees were most fortunate in working for a company whose labour relations policy was years ahead of its time. Mond, a man who found it difficult to establish friendly relationships as an individual, had the most benevolent and progressive ideas when it came to maintaining healthy co-operation with the workforce and his policy has continued ever since.

The Wall Street crash ruined substantial companies and even giants such as ICI were rocked to their foundations. Mond, or Lord Melchett as he now was, leaned on old friendships to inject liquid capital into the company. Melchett died in 1930, when ICI were still struggling to climb out of the morass of a world slump. But it was his belief in the value of research and development that was to help make ICI great once more.

The Plastic Age

It was ICI who, in the thirties, launched the first successful thermoplastic products onto the world market. It was their belief in extensive research and the enlisting of the best brains in the research and development business which gave us what is now generally termed polythene. In 1939 its full scope had not been determined, but war is always a great accelerator. Radar, just being developed, was in dire need of a super-efficient insulator, and polythene filled the bill perfectly. There is no doubt that the success of Watson-Watt's radar would have been greatly reduced without the benefit of ICI's discovery. Another plastic product which timed its advent remarkably well for successful wartime use was 'Perspex'. The first Spitfire in 1936 with its 'Perspex' windscreen and canopy signalled a new era for the warplanes to follow.

That other momentous episode unfolding when war began and hastened by it – nuclear fission – could not have taken up any laboratory space or time without ICI's involvement. 'Tube alloys' had nothing directly to do with tubes or alloys, but the mere words will convey a wealth of meaning to those on the inside at ICI in the war years.

At the end of the war, when there was no established domestic nuclear industry, ICI was the only company capable of designing a feasible atomic energy plant. Atlee's government put paid to (Lord) McGowan's patriotic and proud hopes on that score by setting up the independent UK Atomic Energy Authority, but it was a chief engineer of ICI's Alkali Division, Christopher Hinton, who was to become a key figure in that future programme.

Plastics, pharmaceuticals and pesticides are but a very few of ICI's achievements, but if we have to leave out all but the landmarks in their short history, we cannot overlook their record in conservation.

Brixham – Place of Prevention

A policy laid down by Brunner, Mond in the beginning has been a priority with ICI ever since. Their outlook and positive, creative activity in conservation is effective in every business unit and in every plant across the world. How many companies have set up an entire establishment for the sole purpose of research and development into ecology and conservation?

ICI did just that.

Today no company, big or small, can afford to transgress legislation or fall below the standards set up to maintain an acceptable level whereby the industry can work within the environment efficiently but with the minimum adverse effects upon that environment. At Brixham, ICI's workers are concerned with nothing but that. Brixham's laboratories opened in 1948 after ICI had become the world's biggest paint manufacturer. Being no longer involved in marine paint problems, the laboratory is now the centre of the ICI Group's worldwide environmental research. Today Brixham's boffins, in addition to a much wider research into the effects of chemicals upon aquatic life, also investigate gaseous emissions, the treatment of waste, disposal methods, industrial water supply sources, and the treatment and prevention of accidental chemical spillage. The sciences Brixham uses for these programmes include biology, physics and chemistry, mathematics and oceanography. In addition to the usual microscopes and computers they also use hovercraft and boats.

There is an historical precedent for industry siting its factories at estuaries and seaports and Brixham is the ideal site for ICI's researches. There they have for some years been harnessing the natural biodegradation process for the treatment of waste. Most organic wastes are broken down satisfactorily by bacteria and other naturally-occurring micro-organisms.

If you are sailing off Brixham, enjoying the picturesque seascape with its fishing boat trawling nearby, take another look at the fishing boat. If it is a particularly efficient and sophisticated vessel with a tall, tubular, girder frame at the stern, the chances are it is not just another one of Devon's many stern trawlers. It could well be *Portunus*, ICI's laboratory trawler, taking samples of seawater or the sea bed, or both. Or – watch out for the signals at the masthead – they may be putting a diver down. Farther up river you may see a small hovercraft buzzing around the mudflats. It's not just aimlessly joyriding, that too is working for ICI by taking samples of sand and mud and small marine life. The discharge of effluent and wastes into coastal waters and estuaries is influenced by tidal forces and weather changes. The oceanography section at Brixham examines all aspects of this and is a constant source of advice upon the treatment and method of all such discharges.

North Sea oil platforms, local authority sewage disposal

schemes, fire brigades dealing with accidental chemical spillages –
all have profited and continue to improve their services because of
Brixham's work. Like that other great body, BP Environmental
Services, ICI at Brixham don't just confine their work to company
activities, worldwide as they are. Other companies and public
authorities know they have a source of top flight professional advice
at Brixham whenever they are faced with problems of conservation
and ecology.

Alfred Mond would have thoroughly approved.

Rulers of the Waves

Man, forever inventive, was trying to produce a working submarine 370 years ago. Then it was royalty – James I – who tried out a rowing boat running on wheels on the bed of the Thames. In the days when heads were as likely to roll as wheels perhaps it didn't seem all that intrepid. Maybe he saw it as an invisible means of escape should it be needed, but history does not record how long he planned to hold his breath under water.

More practical by a long chalk was the invention of a Mr Garret, a Liverpool curate, in 1879. His vessel worked, to a degree anyway. It actually travelled underwater for 12 miles before needing to surface. Its propulsion method – a steam boiler where evaporation of the steam gave pressure to turn a screw – was the drawback. It was a pretty hazardous thing to take underwater with you in a sealed container. The boiler after all did need a furnace. It was John P. Holland, of the good old US of A, who eventually came up with the final parent design. His company, suitably named the Electric Boat Company, still builds subs for the US Navy today. Nuclear now of course, but in 1900 Holland boats had the right formula: electric motors to drive the boats underwater, petrol engines to provide drive on the surface and – more importantly – to recharge the batteries. Our own Navy, under pressure, placed an order with Vickers for a Holland–type submarine in 1901 and with the experience of building five of those in a year (five in one year?!) Vickers designed and built their own sub in 1902. A hundred feet long, she was half as big again as the Holland class. The first submarine had a very chequered career. She was severely damaged in a surface collision in 1904. While being towed to the breaker's yard in 1913 she sank off the Eddystone lighthouse – and lay there until discovered by the minesweeper HMS *Bossington* in 1981. This piece of sub-aquatic history is now at the submarine museum at Gosport. But when submarine No.1 left the slipway at Walney Island in 1902 she was to prove a remarkable design. 'At last', it was reported of her after sea trials, 'a submarine that can run at full speed (7 knots), steering by periscope for 6 miles at a depth of 12 feet'! The great breakthrough here was achieving this without the fearful vibration previously set up by the periscope.

HMS *Upholder*, last of one tradition and first of another, followed the same launching path as her grand ancestor eighty years before her. 230 feet long and 2,400 tonnes, she can travel over 2000 nautical miles, spend twenty-eight days on patrol at that radius and still return the 2,000 miles to base. And all this at a

Preparing the Launching for H.M.S. Upholder - Walney. 1986

submerged depth of 500 feet plus, only coming up to 'snort' depth for battery charging. Yes, battery charging. Vickers Shipbuilding and Engineering is well experienced in the design and construction of nuclear–powered hunter killers, but *Upholder* is a diesel electric. In a day when 'Nuke' and 'Sub' are synonymous it may be a surprise to learn this fact. A 'conventional' warfare weapon may be a reassurance for some, but she carries a 'weapons fit' comparable to the latest nuclear powered subs.

For this totally new diesel electric design the Navy followed tradition and revived an old name: Upholder was last used on a World War II sub that built up a reputation second to none, gaining an illustrious record in the early days of the war and a VC for her captain, Lt Commander Malcolm D. Wanklyn, before the inevitable law of averages brought her (and her commander) to the bottom of the sea forever, in the Mediterranean in April 1942.

A proud name, a proud ship and a proud company. It is a company that has been building ships for over a hundred years, and

THE LAUNCHING OF HMS UPHOLDER.

I sensed rather than saw any signs of nostalgia when I watched from close quarters this last slipway launching from Vickers' Walney Island shipyard. This initially slow and suspenseful, stern-first slide of the vessel into the water and then the smooth acceleration of movement with the clatter of chain and cables has always been a great spectator event.

The impact upon and the displacement of thousands of tons of seawater creates a temporary reverse tidal wave back up the slipway and the surprising realisation that already the ship, a hand's touch away moments ago, is now a hundred yards out in the tideway, current swinging the stern and tug controlling the stem.

I suppose when the next submarine is sitting on the dry hard of VSEL's new ship-build yard waiting for the sluices to open and the water to flood in and float her on its surface, the occasion will still be quite an event – but it won't be the same, will it?
Watercolour and acrylic, 15" × 22"

not only for this country. It is anticipated that the new Upholder class will find buyers in the Middle and Far East.

Vickers' shipyard at Barrow has always had up-to-date production facilities, but currently they are completing a massive new shipyard complex. They speak of it as a 'ship build facility' but it still seems a mundane, if not inadequate, title for such a massive construction scheme. Phase I saw the building of an assembly shop extension covering nearly 5,000 square yards and just about 39 yards high. Just one part of Phase II saw 1.5 million tons of sand pumped into Devonshire Dock to provide more land at water level and, finally, the finished construction hall covers 27,000 square yards of ground, with a towering height of over 55 yards.

The great roof will support radio-controlled overhead cranes, each with a lifting capacity of over 150 tonnes. The transfer system covering the whole floor conveys the complete submarine out into the adjacent shiplift. 177 yards long and capacity 24,000 tonnes, it is the heaviest-rated shiplift in the world. The traditional launch, rushing down the slipway, will be no more. Future submarines will drop gently – at about one foot per minute – into their natural element.

These facilities provide work for 2,500 – 3,000 employees. And on the next launch they won't be looking at their watches and tide tables – the new 'facility' need not wait upon tides and slipways. Now *that* I do call enterprise, it's not often man can cock a snook at the tides!

Spreading the Word on a Grand Scale

THE POST OFFICE AND BRITISH RAIL

I didn't know that the first class stamp I put on my letters meant the likelihood of them travelling airmail – not, that is, until I visited Derby airport.

The East Midlands Airport was kind to me that bleak night in late November. Well, at that time of the year, with the vagaries of British weather, it should at least have been very cold. It could too have been very wet and very windy – might even have been snowing. Fortunately, it was none of these things through the midnight hours I spent there watching the largest transport 'hub' operation in the country. One section of the airport is taken over entirely by the Post Office and air traffic controllers are busy with eighteen aircraft coming in from different parts of the country, carrying nothing but UK first class mail. While the original sorting of the mail directing it to this operation centre is largely electronically controlled and computer linked and the aircraft are all flying with modern radar navigation aids, this actual night's work that I watched was highly labour intensive. The hangar-type building that was the central receiving depot for some million letters and packages held too the staff necessary physically to handle that amount of material.

There was a moving conveyor belt taking mailbags from inside to outside loading ramps. But the sheer bulk of the mail could be coped with only by muscle-power when it came to loading it into the wire caged trucks to be towed out and transferred to the waiting aircraft. Similarly, unloading delivery aircraft required the same manoeuvre.

What makes this a 'hub' operation is its crucially timed linking with road and rail services. The rail service is of course the famous Travelling Post Office or TPO.

Whilst the airport night operation was getting underway I left to visit Derby station and observe the arrival of two TPOs, one from Newcastle and one from St Pancras, London. On most nights they arrive on time and a proud, punctual arrival that immediately sparks off a hive of industry seems to give the grimy, characterless diesel locomotives some drama and atmosphere they normally lack. The trains shudder to a halt exactly opposite each other with just the double platform between them. All the sorting and bagging has been done aboard the TPOs whilst they thundered through the night carrying only Post Office sorting staff, several million letters and a few thousand mailbags. By the time the TPO arrives at Derby station the bags have swallowed all the letters; they have been

HIGH SPEED TPO
Even with the much derided and mundane diesel there is still enough spectacle in a British Rail locomotive travelling at high speed to bring out the dormant schoolboy in most men. With the unbroken banner of scarlet Royal Mail livery streaming behind it, this locomotive lacks only its headplume of steam to match the excitement of a bygone age.
Watercolour sketch, 15" × 22"

checked, sealed and labelled and are pounced upon by Derby Post Office's night shift, who then either transfer them to other TPOs or dispatch them on Post Office vans for delivery to the East Midlands Airport.

To the uninitiated the scene must look like the Great Train Robbery all over again – not only duplicated, but gone stark staring mad. Each train is being emptied at a frantic pace with little electric trolleys towing long trains of mini mail wagons at alarming speed. Many of them are disappearing down the underground ramp heading for waiting vans outside, others are zigzagging from platform to platform. Realisation dawns that this high-speed and highly efficient uniformed gang, having emptied both trains, is now loading some of its haul back into the trains again! But not the same train the load was 'hijacked' from – that is the secret. I had to be quick on my feet that night. The ferrying trolleys had one aim in mind: to get the job done. The little bevy of highly placed Post Office executives with me made no difference, those little trains were no respecters of persons. The highly placed executives had to demonstrate as much nifty footwork as myself; the hour was late

and so was one of the TPOs and the night shift was intent on making up lost time.

British Rail are contracted to both provide and operate TPOs, and to run them to 'suitable schedules'. Part of the efficiency of this hub operation is thus dependant upon factors other than Post Office capabilities.

Is it somehow indicative of the British nature that many a workforce pursuing its occupation in extreme conditions will do so with particular vigour and pride? Certainly this was evident on the cold windswept tarmac of the Derby airport, and equally so at 1.00am at the city's station. The 'leaves on the line' reason presented by British Rail for the late arrival of one TPO was greeted with frustrated annoyance by Post Office staff, not just because it was going to make them all late off shift, but because they took a pride in operating an efficient service.

With other services apart from nearly forty TPOs, there are some 3,000 trains being used by the Post Office on the British Rail network. Such involvement in a system so prone to industrial dispute and weather problems must be a consistent challenge to its organisers.

MIDNIGHT MAIL AT DERBY AIRPORT
This study for the large oil canvas that followed still conveys, with its briefly scribbled lines and quick dashes of colour, the intense activity that I beheld that November night: planes taking off, planes landing and planes taxiing in an apparently haphazard fashion and yet with obvious professional control and intention.

The object here was to land as soon as safety permitted, load or unload their cargoes of mailbags and return as quickly as possible to their various destinations. The scores of Post Office workers with their 'mini-trains' timed their arrivals so that their wagons were alongside aircraft loading doors almost before engine shut-off. It was a fascinating example of total work efficiency.
Wash and pen – study for oil, 22" × 30"

Mount Pleasant underground railway:
beating the traffic jams across
London.
Watercolour, 15" ×22"

The PO's Private Underground Railway

The more I investigate postal activity the more I discover how
dependant over the past century communication has been upon
transport. Despite the telephone, radio, telex and satellite
communications people all over the world still write to one another
and all their letters amount daily to a phenomenal weight.

Having looked at the major means of transport – vans, trains
and aircraft – used by the Post Office, I turned my attention to
another system. This was planned in the early 1900s but had to wait
for the intervention of World War I before being finally built just
sixty years ago. Oh yes, it's still wheels, but wheels with a
difference: small solid iron wheels, wheels that Brunel would have
approved of, as he would the locomotives and carriages they carry
from one side of London to the other.

Whilst the Police cope with the daily nightmare of the traffic
sandwiched between Paddington and Whitechapel which grinds to
a near halt regularly three times a day, 50,000 bags of London's post
are being transported swiftly and without any holdups on a
miniature railway 70 feet below those smelly, noisy, maddening
thoroughfares. The Post Office underground railway is an absolute

delight for those enthusiasts of Basset-Lowke and Hobbies. It is a miniature railway guaranteed to turn all grown men instantly into small boys again. Venture into its main depot at Mount Pleasant (taking a lift that transports you lower than the deepest London Transport underground line) and you enter another world, a world that has echoes of Victoriana. Its technology seems to have stayed somewhere between the two world wars, yet it is a technology that is super-efficient. Such an electric system demands an efficient control room and the control room here is no exception, yet it is surprisingly compact and simple in its function. It has good solid 1920s slide controls, strong mild steel with ebonite handles, to select and change routes. No sign here of plastic, electronic controls or computer ware. Direct linkage, solid brass and steel; what worked well in 1927 works better than well sixty years later. The only concession to a later age is an illuminated facsimile of the track system – scaled down of course – a six-foot panel representing part of the six and a half miles of track.

Little blue dots of light represent each train, following its movement on the lines. But if the controls are simple here the relay rooms hold bank upon bank of fuses, relays and cutouts, massive copper-bladed cutouts that need a strong right hand to operate. There are solenoids that look as if they could trip out half of London's lights. The blue flashes of arcing light occurring as various contacts open and close are not startling, they seem totally appropriate to this prewar store of heavy-duty electrics – not electronics, mind.

The controls have all lasted and served their sixty years well and look as if they are capable of another sixty. The locomotives and wagons they govern, though small, are solidly built. Standing little more than 4 feet high but 25 feet long, the engines are self-driven. There are no footplates or guards on these trains, they spurn any human intrusion, obeying only the electric impulse from the control room. Not long ago a visiting inspector decided the machines could be updated. He sniffed at the sight of the massive cart-type leaf springs on the engines and decided they could be remodelled with modern hydraulic suspension. Some prototypes were put into service. After a few months Mount Pleasant's well-equipped workshops grew tired of continually having to service and repair them. The modern suspension proved no match for the heavy workload imposed upon it. The modern hybrids were consigned to the workshop stores, to be broken up for spare parts. The men continued lovingly to tend the sixty-year-old little giants with old fashioned grease guns and plenty of polish and the modern designers of the twentieth century were taught a lesson in basic engineering.

If you get into one of those frustrating traffic jams around St Paul's and you realise that no way are you going to get to Paddington Station in time for your train, then think of those stout little engines 70 feet below you. They will have done the trip, with six stops, and be on the return journey long before you get there. If you have posted some first class mail that day at least it will be some consolation. Unfortunately, you can't rush down there and shorten your own journey – it's strictly post only, no passengers.

Greenbat Limited of Leeds built the latest trains when replacements were needed and services increased, but they still build them to the same basic design.

I have always been a devout fan of J. M. W. Turner – but what has that to do with the Post Office underground railway? Remember that World War I interrupted the building of that railway? Well, the tunnels were dug and finished in 1914. These 9-foot caverns dwarf the mini trains, but the bombproof tunnels served as splendid safe deposits for those superb Turner canvases from the Tate Gallery and other paintings from the National Portrait Gallery, thus frustrating the Kaiser's Zeppelins. Well done Post Office! Such preservation for posterity is forever honoured in the great annals of painting.

Such foresight was also evident, most remarkably so, when those early planners of 1911 prepared a report (today we would call it a feasibility study) upon the planned railway in which we read, '...Even with motorised vans the average speed for cross-London traffic (surface) will not rise above 8mph...' How right they were!

Despite all this, for most of us the Post Office is represented by that one simple act of collecting and delivering that letter we have just stuck a stamp on. Yes, some of us do remember when there was a 'same day' London service, when a letter posted this afternoon would always reach Uncle Fred in Manchester tomorrow morning – and nine times out of ten it still will. But that was over forty years ago, when a letter was an event to the average family, when commercially solicited mail shots were unknown, when even the busy Christmas card deliveries averaged little more than ten per family. But – and this is the crunch fact – today *11,000 million*, yes, eleven thousand million, letters go through the Post Office's sorting offices in a year. There's only one answer to handling such a mammoth load of merchandise, and, yes, you've guessed it: extend that splendid underground railway to all the major provincial towns and cities!

Bell, Book and Cable

BRITISH TELECOM

British Telecom is all about communications. If you want to trace its historic beginnings you have to go back to the days of Marconi, Edison and Bell and really to appreciate the progress made we have to go back to the first telephone line ever installed. Which one was that? There isn't an easy answer, and we *do* have to join Bell in the past to get anywhere near it.

When the Scotsman Alexander Graham Bell came back to this country from America where his demonstration of the new invention had been ecstatically received, he met a more critical reception. Some were fascinated with it, some saw it as a great breakthrough in communication and others dismissed it as useless trickery. In those early days it was an expensive item to add to a household so it comes as no surprise to learn that it was the landed gentry of the day who were the early customers.

Britain was ever the home of entrepreneurs ever ready to cash in on new inventions. Patents were easily flouted in those days and various small companies soon set up in business producing near copies of Bell's apparatus. These sold to local squires and landowners who were pleased to flaunt the facility of ringing the head groom in his stable den from the lavish comfort of their library and ordering the horse or carriage.

Those early internal lines arrived about 1878 and Queen Victoria was given a demonstration of similar equipment at Osborne House that same year. Who could claim to have installed the first of those simple in-house phones we don't know, but there *is* a claimant to the first proper telephone exchange, which is far more relevant to the industry's history. In August 1879 the first public exchange was set up in London to deal with the capital's telephone subscribers. It had eight lines, one of which went to the home of the company chairman. A far cry from the recent announcement of British Telecom's *22 millionth* line being installed!

Today we are used to the sight of Telecom engineers, either repairing or installing one of the thousands of cables that lie beneath our streets. What we don't see is the vast network of cables that lie under the oceans. Though satellites cover the world for urgent immediate communication, visual and sound, the underwater cables still carry a vast amount of telephone traffic. Like their counterparts in other industries they too are updating their technology. The use of optical fibres, a science in itself, has transformed the capabilities of British Telecom's communications

CABLES TO THE SEABED
British Telecom's automatic underwater cable layer, the 'Plough'.
Acrylic and wash colour, 22" × 15"

cables. As its name might suggest, an optical fibre cable is a fraction of the size of a standard coaxial cable. The first ever international optical fibre cable was laid in 1986, between Broadstairs in Kent and Ostend, Belgium. Just three pairs of optical fibres carry no less than 12,000 digital circuits. The older, heavy coaxial cable could transmit not much more than 4,000 circuits. Denmark will soon be similarly linked with the UK in 1988 and the UK with North America will follow shortly after.

To create this seabed system of communication British Telecom has for some years run its own specialised fleet of ships. Maintenance alone has kept them constantly busy and now, to cope with new demands, one of the three cable laying ships, the *Alert,* has had a £2 million refit; this makes it one of the most versatile and up-to-date vessels of this type in the world. One of the *Alert's* 'tools' is the 'Plough'. Developed by BT, it is a £1 million product that makes the job of laying undersea cables both quicker and more efficient. It is well named because it does in effect do just that: automatically it ploughs a furrow through the sea bed, but then continues to lay the cable a good yard deep and cover up the trench when the cable is laid. It is just as efficient too at recovering the cable for maintenance purposes. The days of telephone cables lying deep on the sea floor being scooped up by fishing trawls or fouled by ships' anchors will soon be a thing of the past.

But of course British Telecom is still largely thought of in the context of the public telephone system as it visually appears to the man in the street. Those of us who regret the passing of the familiar red phone boxes have to accept the need somehow to combat the needless vandalism of our society. Currently, 77,000 old favourites are being replaced with fully glazed stainless steel booths, which it is hoped will reduce the annual £20 million damage repair bill. To old-fashioned tastes the new booths may be just another product of the functional modern style that seems to display so little imagination on the part of its designers. But what happened to the wheelchair-bound with our old boxes? Nothing: they could never make a phone call from the street. In the new ones they *can.*

Over the next six years almost all 78,300 public payphones will be replaced, at a cost of £160 million. But the nostalgic will be pleased to know that there will be a handful of the old red favourites still scattered around. In certain conservation areas where sensitive local authorities try to preserve the best of the old, British Telecom are leaving some. If you find one in years to come, just keep mum about it. Don't let the mindless ones know of its whereabouts.

Talking of phone boxes inevitably brings thoughts of the 999 call. I remember the fanfare of publicity when this was introduced, and find it hard to believe Telecom when they tell me it's been with us for fifty years! In 1937 the London exchange, first to be fitted with it, endured a deafening klaxon and a large flashing red lamp whenever anyone dialled the three alarm digits. It's a little less brutal in its warning to the operator now. All 999 calls are automatically recorded for future reference and the modern communications systems with computerised call-out to fire services means a full briefing in seconds to whichever service is required.

The volume of calls inland increased by 7 per cent; internationally, there was an increase of 11 per cent. A new exchange system is being commissioned each day and there are 250 small rural exchanges in operation now. With all this increase in their services it's nice to know that 90 per cent of the work BT has to place with outside contractors goes to British companies, and 60 per cent of that to small and medium-sized firms. If those turnover and profit figures seemed large, measure against them the fact that in one year (1987) £190 million was spent on research and development.

British Telecom microwave tower, Isle of Man
Acrylic, wash colour and pen,
22"×15"

A Metalsome Industrial Giant

THE BRITISH STEEL CORPORATION

At the end of 1980, the giant British Steel Corporation seemed but a shadow of its former self, its present unhappy and its future in doubt. The workforce was reduced to 129,000, half its 1967 total. Where pre-energy crisis optimism had forecast a yearly target of up to 36 million tonnes, 1980's capacity became 15 million.

In the face of such market forces and labour-cum-union pressures, few industrial leaders could have survived, let alone proceeded with measures conceived in far happier times. BSC chairman Ian MacGregor and his deputy Bob Scholey were, however, as strong as the steel they worked for. They persisted in a total reorganisation and cost cutting that could prove eventually to be the only sure way of not just saving an industry but of putting it firmly on a new path of successful production. The three-month strike in 1980, caused by pay disputes and the antagonism of the unions towards radical change, at its end revealed a more understanding labour force no longer striking over principles, but accepting the need to slim down the workforce. Plans for restructuring were not shelved through that period, they continued operating. The measures set in train long before continued. The age-old stigma of being unemployed has lost some of its sting in today's society and the scale of compensation handed out at the end of the day must have gone a long way to making it bearable. Thousands of workers received the equivalent of a two-year pay packet. The very smallest payout was over £6000.

Under MacGregor's direction the overweight and out-of-date giant BSC continued the process of slimming and abandoning outmoded and restrictive work practices. Over that last decade the treatment had been painful, at times traumatic but above all necessary. The real tragedy was that it had not happened earlier.

There is no crystal ball that can predict an industry's future, but at least British Steel is now on level terms with most of the competition. From what I saw of activities in its plants it is now a very healthy giant, thriving on that competition.

BSC Shotton

In the early 70s, as part of the new, restructured British Steel Corporation, Shotton embarked, as did every other division, upon its ten-year development programme. This decade brought with it the most far-reaching upheavals of its entire history. When the dust of the 1980 strike had settled and management had clearly chosen its path there were few options left for the workforce. For the 6,500

Charging with scrap.
Acrylic and watercolour, 22"×15"

made redundant there was a shareout of £65 million – no substitute perhaps for continuing employment, but far more than they would have dared expect had BSC not been a member of the European steel industries readaptation scheme. But, give Shotton its due, it did not rest upon those financial laurels. When the end of the old world came, side by side with the redundancy payments everyone was given expert counselling. No man went away clutching his temporary wealth without the benefit of professional advice on how best to use both the money and his own personal talents in whatever future lay before him.

The painful surgery over and done, recovery has been satisfactory, if slow. In Shotton, where once stood the mighty blast furnaces and sinter plants, now flourishes a thriving paper mill.

Overleaf

Hot strip mill at Port Talbot
Acrylic and watercolour, 15"×22"

There are 250 new jobs on site, with fruitful spinoffs for the forestry industry of nearby North Wales and increased demand for the heavy transport industry. A hundred acres of unwanted land was handed over to the Welsh Land Development Agency and further areas surplus to the new requirements were given to Clwyd County Council. Subsequently the new Garden City project, fostered and developed by joint authorities, has furnished another 4,000 jobs in the area.

Conservation and Ecology

One of the steelwork's lakes, which was once a source of cooling water for the hot metal processes, has now been cleaned out and restored to provide a winter home for the thousands of terns on their migratory path from Scandinavia. It was heartwarming to find such caring in an environment where the major product was soulless, the weather bleak and the natives necessarily a tough breed. I had thought that wildlife conservation could be a forgotten cause in an area where human beings were still restructuring their own traumatised lives. Not so. Not only was the lake given over to the terns but, using specially constructed rafts, artificial islands were created in the middle of the lake, giving the birds a more secure and easily defended nesting site.

Yet another lake, larger still, became a centre for leisure activity – sailing and angling – and simple natural beauty was restored. I thus could see the evidence of restructuring even before I stepped inside the production plants of Shotton.

The New Plant

My slight knowledge of recent history should have prepared me for the first impression I received, but I was still surprised at the degree of automation at Shotton. The workforce is now 2,200 – not an inconsiderable number of beings if you lined them all up – but they were spread pretty thinly over the ground. Shiftwork and what is still a pretty large site seem to reduce that number to a visible handful.

In the cold strip mill, a giant barn-like building, hundreds of coils of strip steel, recently arrived from Ravenscraig, are lined up looking like fearful ammunition for some unseen weapon of war. These shining coils, 5-6 feet diameter and up to 4 feet wide, weigh variously from 12 to 32 tonnes each. There they stand, row upon silent row, with just the occasional worker moving around and checking them for process and destination.

That plant is the first stage where the coils of raw material come in. 'Pickled' clean and rolled down to desired thickness, it then goes through various processes to finish up as customer-ready, polished steel, galvanised or coated.

In June 1986 a new £30 million plant was opened that not only produces the conventional hot dip galvanised strip (Galvatite) but a new product for BSC, an aluminium/zinc alloy-coated strip (Zalutite). (History will certainly not record a reluctance of management to invest capital into the production side through these years.) The £30 million spent on the new coating line was followed in December of the same year with an £18 million refurbishment of the electro-zinc plating line.

Cold strip mill, Shotton.
Watercolour and acrylic, 15"x22"

When the 1980 agreement on new 'slimline' restructuring was reached it was based on production targeting of 10,000–12,500 tonnes per week and a workforce reduced from 4,200 to 3,350. At the end of 1986 production had risen to an average *15,000* tonnes per week with a workforce not of 3,350 but 2,230. And that 15,000 tonnes is not being stockpiled waiting for orders. Nearly every finished coil of steel, Galvatite, Zalutite and Stelvetite that comes off the end of the line is labelled, ready and waiting for customer delivery.

Britain's steel industry has been both the victim and the conqueror of history's evolutionary process. Political influences can never be ignored, world affairs must certainly be monitored and social obligations do not end at the factory gates. Constant awareness of those factors and keeping abreast of technology is now, one feels, an inherited policy that will be its strongest defence against the shocks of history.

It is a paradox of the modern steel industry that the more successful its production technology becomes the more competitive, if not difficult, becomes the life of its producers.

In Europe, fortunately, it was recognised quite early on that in an industry that counts its weekly production in tens of thousands of tonnes, there would have to be an agreement on quotas. This would at least prevent any mammoth corporation swamping the market, with its accompanying economic confusion. But it still remained a market that had no place for the timorous.

In March 1986 new chairman Bob Scholey told BSC: 'This year is make or break!' This followed a £370 million capital expenditure programme. (The estimated level of capital expenditure per annual turnover necessary for any steel company to remain viable is 7 per cent, which shows the enormity of the figures involved in this industry.) By the November of that same year he was able to report a *profit* of £68 million for the half-year. March 1987 saw that increased to £178 million for the year. That figure was still short of the £300 million British Steel forecast would be needed to maintain it as a viable market force – but an astonishing turnround from 1979's loss of £1.8 billion.

At one time it was enough in business to make a profit. What pressures world markets and economics place upon a home industry!

BSC Teesside

Teesside, having been an established home of heavy industry since the days of Stephenson and Watt, still conveys to the first time visitor the picture of an industry-dominated landscape. The one-time home of iron mining, with its long involvement in shipbuilding, iron and steel that dates back to Bessemer, is imbued with an air of harsh reality. This is industrial country. There is no hiding it.

The modern blast furnace that stands as high as St Paul's recently went into its second campaign. That industrial jargon simply means that it has virtually been demolished and rebuilt. A modern blast furnace is never, for sheer economic reasons, allowed to go out during a campaign, which can last more than twelve years. Sometimes, for the briefest of periods, it might be 'damped down'. Finally, the refractory linings of the furnace eventually fall below their required standard, as do other components, and have to be replaced.

Redcar's steelmen still talk enthusiastically about the furnace replacement. When they installed the furnace in 1979, it was a massive project. Japanese steel engineers, way ahead in their

Big 'B'
Acrylic and watercolour, 22″ × 15″

experience of 'refurnacing' in those days, came over to advise and assist. The size of the job was such that some six months was reckoned to be the realistic time required to complete it.

In 1986 there was a new air of co-operative enthusiasm. 'We can beat the Japanese time' was a bold but confident statement. And they did. The biggest blast furnace in Europe was demolished, rebuilt and relit in 135 days.

But there aren't just furnaces at Teesside. From its docks one can follow the progress of raw ores and fuels arriving and then going

through the various processes. Having watched one of British
Steel's own giant ore carriers unloading and then, within an easy
rail wagon's shunting distance, 32-tonne steel slabs nearly 10 yards
long coming off the roller tables in the Universal Beam mill you
begin to realise what a tremendous advantage it is to have every
process from beginning to end carried out on one site. Given that
facility, plus some of the most up-to-date technology in the business,
the management of a past era might have sat complacently back
waiting for orders.

Naked heat: the power of the electric arc furnace
Acrylic and watercolour, 15" × 22"

But not the management of today. With world production capacities well in excess of current demand throughout Europe, Japan and America, BSC concentrates on high standards of quality and delivery in a fiercely competitive market. Danny Ward, Teesside director and thirty-four years in the industry, wears no rose-tinted spectacles, but his realistic outlook is coupled with a firm confidence in his workforce. Teesside teaches them, trains them*, gives them a production bonus-sharing scheme, promotes them from the floor and – in short – treats them like the reasonable, intelligent human beings they are. And they respond accordingly. On Teesside man hours per tonne of output have improved in five years from 14 hours to *3.8* hours.

Old hands talked to me proudly of present records and shook their heads over past history. 'We've got seven and a half thousand men here now producing 3 million tonnes of steel annually – a few years back we had difficulty achieving that between Consett, Hartlepool and here with twenty-five thousand men or more...' Admittedly, the increased technology and the massive investment have produced a more streamlined, efficient plant, but on my limited acquaintance I would hesitate to pinpoint a cause for the very apparent optimism and pride among the workers themselves. Perhaps it was always there and just wanted re-awakening.

*Like the other British Steel plants, Teesside has its own Open Learning, on-site training scheme.

Selby, the New Face of Coal

BRITISH COAL

*O*ne particularly famous coal seam that runs through west and south Yorkshire is the Barnsley seam, a rich underground river of coal that has supported the prosperity of the area's coalfields for more than a century. Rich though it was, it appeared to peter out when it reached north in the Selby area, a low-lying rural landscape straddling the River Ouse. In 1904 test boreholes showed a sudden reduction in quality and quantity. The Barnsley seam was not to yield up its rich product to the colliers of North Yorkshire, at least not for another sixty years or more. The rural landscape stayed rural and the Ouse continued to irrigate the countryside. To the south came the needed power stations to cope with the twentieth century's ever-increasing demand for electrical power. Ferrybridge, Eggborough and Drax were environmental intrusions that people learned to live with and, at least, an area of some 100 square miles north-east of the Ouse stayed green and clean. No gaunt, black headframes with their spinning wheels and colliers' cages dominated this scene. The sheep still grazed and the fields were green, not black. It was 1967 when Coal Board geologists, following the oldest scientific evidence of all, a hunch, found that those earlier test borings had been at fault and not the coal seam. The 'Barnsley' *was* there, as rich and abundant as a century ago, just waiting to be worked. It was ironical that, in that same year, coal mines all over Europe were closing and oil, the great energy provider, was boasting of its success as the cheaper and more abundant supplier. Then international greed and foreign manipulation somehow reversed the coin and in less than six years we had an energy crisis. Now it transpired the research people of the Coal Board had not just bided their time, they had used it wisely: a report was immediately available showing the very worthwhile and viable potential of the new Selby coalfield. On reflection, perhaps it was just as well that history had marked time on this coal development for so long.

Of course, in 1975 nobody just opened up a new coal mine – no matter how much it was needed. Initial planning application met with inquiries that lasted three months. The conservationists were no longer just 'green' pressure group enthusiasts. Government and the governed had learned that environmental safeguards were a necessity, not just a grudging compromise. By the time all these factors had exerted their influence and HRH the Duchess of Kent had ceremonially started the first drilling near the little village of Wistow in 1976, a remarkable new chapter of Yorkshire coalmining had begun.

Selby Abbey, supported on a pillar of coal
Wash and pen, 22" × 15"

The Selby Concept

There were to be six collieries in the new Selby coalfield, but only five of them were to produce coal. The sixth, Gascoigne Wood, has no working coal face of its own, and yet is the biggest site in the whole field and its function is really the key to the whole project. Gascoigne Wood is both the beginning and the end of the rich Selby coalfield. It's a 'drift' mine at the surface of two 7½-mile underground tunnels. With a gradient of 1 in 4 to begin with, these tunnels level off to become underground spine roads forming

Titan at work. Tunneling at Selby.
Watercolour and acrylic, 22" ×30"

junctions as they meet with the deeper coal-producing mines of Wistow, Whitemoor, Riccall, Stillingfleet and North Selby. Those mines will no longer bear the burden of handling, cleaning, loading and transporting the coal in addition to mining it. Once cut from the face (by power loading shearers) underground 'roadways' from each mine, linked to the spine tunnels, will transfer the coal automatically to the powerful conveyor belts which transport it up to Gascoigne Wood.

The Barnsley seam coal is top quality, just right for power station consumption, and a few miles away are three of the biggest coal-fired power stations in Europe. They will receive a minimum 10,000,000 tonnes a year of Selby's output when all five mines are on stream, and only one form of transport can really cope with that continual demand: rail. The siting of Gascoigne Wood for the 'control' drift mine was deliberately ideal geographically, but

Enterprise on Canvas

another benefit was quite fortuitous; it had been in the distant past the site of a small railway marshalling yard. Selby's planners blessed Dr Beeching and included the old rail beds and hard standings in their layout. New tracks were laid and British Rail will transport the coal direct from the stockyards of Gascoigne Wood to the customers at Eggborough, Drax and Ferrybridge.

Don Haigh, the manager of Gascoigne Wood, is a tough, forthright Yorkshireman. Typical of British Coal's management today, he is a real collier. Thirty-five years in the industry have taken him from pit boy to manager, encompassing nearly every task and experience the industry offers. The one it can still offer, modern safeguards notwithstanding, is tragedy. Don Haigh has had that experience too, for the flooding disaster at the Lofthouse mine, near Wakefield, claimed his miner son. But bitterness, if there is any, doesn't show. The Yorkshire fortitude does, but through it all, undiminished, shines enthusiasm for his job. Fortitude suggests stolid acceptance but, like many of his contemporaries, Haigh has a foresight and adaptability that might have brought mining more quickly into the twentieth century had old company bosses recognised these traits earlier in their employees at the coal face.

The designers responsible for Selby's construction have done a remarkable job too. I thought of the ghastly monstrosities dreamt up by architects in some of our great cities and decided it would be no bad thing to hand over the rebuilding of London to British Coal's industrial architects.

Compliance with conservation demands didn't just end with clever and subtle design of buildings. There is no soil pollution or encroachment to harm the farming community. Sheep still graze right up to the walls of the winding house (which no old Rhondda collier would ever recognise!) and the plough cuts a furrow a few yards from the coal wagons. But all the best ecological intentions could sink, literally, if that bugbear of mining – subsidence – was not guarded against. Selby Abbey, 900 years old, takes precedence over coal, even though the same Barnsley seam runs near it. At safe distances from the Abbey, pillars of the coal face are left, acting as underground supports long before any minor tremors or falls might disturb the vestry. Even the main railway line to York was moved and rebuilt entirely at British Coal's expense to avoid any possible disturbance. Similar precautions protect the actual town of Selby and 'pillaring' is even extended to protect a sensitive area of the river.

A more perceptible, individual appreciation of ecology came our way when our party visited another of Selby's mines, Stillingfleet. Deputy manager Terry Hughes was staring out of his office window when we arrived. The scene outside was quite a verdant one – luxuriant growth, trees, shrubs and plants with wildlife to match. It was the wildlife aspect that excited him: 'It's still there', he said triumphantly and then, in answer to our blank looks, 'The chaffinch – it's been there a week and now it's got a clutch of five eggs in the nest!' As the chaffinch had built its home in a shrub no higher than the window sill, and not fifty feet away from a works access road, we had to share Terry's enthusiasm. Any creature setting up house here on a coal mine needs care and attention or a lot of luck. This one had all three. Its luck was in finding this particular manager's office. The care and attention followed automatically. Perhaps this trusting little bird had done its homework on this particular office prior to nesting?

Apparently there were rabbits in profusion around the site as well. Hares were not uncommon and there was a reported sighting of a deer. At the moment though the chaffinch with its potential young took priority. We agreed that five eggs for a chaffinch was quite a scoring rate, if not a record. On the other hand, with records becoming an expected norm at Selby, perhaps the chaffinch having opted for this environment was simply adopting local custom.

Terry Hughes started his career down the pit as a pony minder. When he briefly related the tale of saving his daily lunch box apple for his pit pony, I wondered how many teenagers had formed an affinity with their four-legged charge, and had shared their lunch box with the animal? Yet there should be no mystery or surprise in finding such industrious grown men personally involved in details of conservation and ecology. When you have spent most of your working life down in the dark confines of a coalpit then the blueness of the sky, the green of the earth and the song of a bird must register far more richly than with those of us who take them so much for granted.

I didn't seek to discuss the politics of mining but, inevitably, the subject of 'the strike' came up. There were details they deplored and lost causes they regretted, but now in retrospect it seemed that the whole affair had been a much needed catalyst. Through better management had come the introduction of radical changes in production methods that would otherwise have taken generations to effect. For the miners the realisation that change could be acceptable, and even beneficial, overcame old loyalties. As with other industries, the diminution of manpower accelerated with the progress of technology and the resultant redundancies were the bitterest of blows to suffer. But as a result the industry in Yorkshire certainly is cleaner, fitter and more productive.

Selby, the plum of modern Yorkshire coalmines, has broken a few records already and looks like breaking many more. During its construction, unique methods were used to conquer nature's obstacles. Water is an ever-present worry in coal mining. Selby, with its low ground level and the dominant River Ouse, is no exception. Modern pumping and sophisticated waterproofing techniques subdue most threats, but at lower levels the engineers came across heavy water ingress in the basal sand strata. Pumping was no answer – but refrigeration was. A series of holes were drilled vertically and refrigerated brine pumped in. It worked like a large-scale domestic freezer. Once frozen, the shafts were driven through, lined and waterproofed. Defrosting then followed and the water-filled basal assumed its normal structure outside and around the coal face.

Giant tunnelling machines were used to drive the two main tunnels through. One of them, the 'Robbins Miner', had a circular cutting head 20 feet in diameter. The conveyor belts that travel endlessly through the two tunnels are the largest in Europe. The production shafts will store between them up to 11,000 tonnes of

AUTOMATIC CUTTER AT THE COAL FACE

Make no mistake, mining in general is still an arduous and hazardous occupation. But the British are world leaders in mining safety and modern mining operations such as are in force at Selby do reduce the hazards and the grime to some considerable degree. Automatic cutters such as this replace the pick and shovel. Powerful, hydraulic roof supports are a world away from the timber pit props and shuttering of yesteryear. But the miner still needs his lamp, and the underground gas seams and water courses still lurk in hiding, waiting to confound the most modern equipment.

Wash and pen, 22" × 15"

coal, while feeding it automatically through to the main conveyor belts.

There are no pit props these days. Hydraulic or powered roof supports in solid steel form roof, floor and side walls, and give the miner a protection unheard of thirty years ago. The pick and shovel has long since been left above ground. Nowadays the 'shearer' takes their place. A revolving cutter, it travels along some 270 yards of coal face, cutting 6 feet deep into the scam and automatically loading onto the conveyor. In just one operation 300 tonnes of coal will be produced every hour. Wistow, as the first Selby mine in production, has already exceeded target figures to such an extent that when the others come on stream the management are predicting the initial 10 million tonnes annual production rate projected is too conservative. 'Twelve million? 15 million?' said Don Haigh. 'You name it – we'll make it'. A super mine costs super money – a billion-pound government loan to be precise. A ten-year clearance of that investment was estimated on the basis of the 10 million tonnes annual production figure for Selby. 'We'll do it before then', said Gascoigne Wood's manager. 'All the other Yorkshire miners are helping us pay off the interest – so we've bloody well got to'.

THE CAGE
Always, no matter how sophisticated and modern, I see the lift that takes the workers down to the pit as a cage. Sombre when it goes down, joyous when it comes to the surface again. That is when you realise that a collier is still a collier in the modern, advanced 20th century. After a spell at the coal face there are still dirty faces and tired eyes and there is still no substitute for the cage to bring them back to God's daylight.
Wash, pen and acrylic, 25" × 17"

Miners checking vertical roof supports.

High-flying Enterprises

BRITISH AEROSPACE

*I*t brings home to us the intense technical drive of this small country of ours to learn that we have one of the largest and most powerful aerospace enterprises in the world. A company engaged in some of the most advanced technology in the world, it employs 76,000 people and *exported* in 1986 over £2 billion worth of its products. We should emphasise that 'over' £2 billion, for the excess is *71 million* – a massive amount in itself.

How did such a company come about in a tiny island that our detractors are constantly knocking as a country sliding down the world scale of prestige? Well, back in yesteryear before the times of oil crises, multi-inflation and international auctions, Britain – like most European countries – relied upon her military air arm being supplied by a number of small aircraft engineering firms. All of them competed to earn contracts from what was often a poorly advised government ministry. Avro, Handley Page, Shorts, Hawker Siddeley, Blackburn, Bristol, Vickers, were but a few. All these names from the early days of powered flight supplied us with warplanes to help bring us through two world wars.

By the seventies, colossal advances in technology plus unbelievable inflation in the cost of materials and labour made survival possible only for the giants of such a specialised industry. In the postwar years the amalgamation of several British aircraft companies gave birth to two groups, the British Aircraft Corporation and Hawker Siddeley aviation, which in turn joined Scottish Aviation to give birth, in 1977, to British Aerospace. It became a public limited company in 1981, and was fully privatised in 1985.

In April 1987 British Aerospace bought from the government the centuries-old Royal Ordnance for the sum of £190 million. Given the government's policy of privatisation, the Royal Ordnance had to go on the market. It was logical that British Aerospace should bid, for they design and make many of the weapons that use the explosives and propellants that the Royal Ordnance produce. It's nice to know though that their new acquisition will still operate under their historic old name. Indeed the Royal Ordnance continues to operate as a wholly-owned subsidiary. The benefits to both will be in the sharing of their research and development programmes and British Aerospace's massive sales presence across the world will be something the ordnance company never enjoyed before.

One of those early names of aviation, Robert Blackburn, founded his company back in 1916. Those were the exciting days

THE NEW SPACE AGE FIGHTER
Still very much a 'hush hush' job, the EAP's appearance gives little away technically. Concealed beneath the streamlined exterior, 'fly-by-wire' technology and modern lightweight materials combine to give function to form. Every line speaks of the cleanest airflow and the minimum drag and for you and me, the laymen, the aircraft gives a picture of sheer speed and graceful beauty. Whether she is a Mach(2) or a Mach(3) fighter we do not know, but it's apparent that the EAP is no slouch!
Watercolour and acrylic, 22" × 30"

of experiment, of trial and error. The Wright Brothers and Bleriot had taken the stage and now many venturesome and inventive enthusiasts were willing to join this new theatre. In a new form of transport that was regarded by the majority as simply crazy or foolhardy, many of its participants were either or both. But Blackburn, if daring, was one of the serious and successful pioneers. His factory at Brough produced a variety of aircraft types over the decades that followed and in 1960 the company joined the famous Hawker Siddeley group. Now the twentieth-century version of the old Blackburn factory is the largest employer on the north Humberside. With 4,500 employees it is one of the largest of British Aerospace's eight military aircraft units. Its production scope is wide: the Harrier of Falklands fame, the Buccaneer and the Phantom are some of our modern front-line aircraft that are worked on at Brough. But though military contracts engage most of their production time, major parts for the European Airbus (the A300 and A310) are also built here. The short haul airliner BAe 146 also has many of its components built here.

In 1986 British Aerospace won *three* Queen's Awards for export achievement, and in the same year launched a revolutionary new fighter plane. This was their own design in a project shared with West Germany and Italy called the Experimental Aircraft Programme.

This Space Age fighter is so new that it has no name, just the 'EAP Demonstrator'. It incorporates many technologies that are so advanced that they had never before been utilised together in one product. Until the EAP they were technologies that had been perfected only individually – waiting for the machine to come along that was capable of using them together. Now that machine has arrived.

Obviously, full details have not been released, but it has been revealed the EAP's wings are built of new carbon fibre composites and that high performance plastics are used in the fuselage. Its engines, fittingly, are Rolls-Royce RB199s. This new technology and materials mean that it is 20 per cent lighter than comparable conventional aircraft. So, obviously, it will take a lot of catching, not only because of its speed but because of its agility.

Another of British Aerospace's advanced research projects really is Space Age. The Hotol (horizontal take off and landing) is a dual-role design. Its conventional method of take off and landing could serve either to send satellites into orbit or, with its phenomenal speed, take City financiers off to a business meeting in Japan. Passengers would board at Heathrow knowing that it was only the 9-hour time lag they had to cope with, for the travel time would be reduced to next to nothing.

British Aerospace seemed comprehensive enough, what with its Airbuses, Space Age fighters, Hotols and its own weapons system. Now that it has the wherewithal to produce its own 'rocket fuel' and 'gunpowder', it really is one of the giants of world aviation.

A Sonic Boom To Success

*T*here are fond memories I cherish – which must seem archaic to others – of boyhood days spent cycling out to Croydon aerodrome to watch the aerial activity of the day. Croydon aerodrome (the term airport was unheard of) was flying's hub of Europe in the early thirties. I used to gaze with awe and excitement at those wonders of aircraft design, Hannibal, Heracles and Helena. Huge, silver bodied, four-engined biplanes built by Handley Page, they were HP42s, claimed to be the world's 'first real airliner'. Ordered by Imperial Airways, they were certainly the first custom built aircraft to operate a regular passenger service in Europe.

In those prewar days, Imperial Airways dominated the runways of the old international airport – sorry, aerodrome – and with the majestic HP42 extended their services through long-distance airmail routes to Karachi and Cairo. This was barely twenty years after Louis Bleriot's first sea-scraping, beach-hopping flight across the English Channel. From Bleriot's flimsy, 30 m.p.h. canvas and wire primitive to Handley Page's 130 m.p.h., 130 foot wingspan, metal clad giant was a monster forward leap in design and construction. This progress owed a lot of course to the imperative demands of the 1914-18 war, but a great deal as well to the foresight and adventuring spirit of those forerunners of today's British Airways.

Within a year or two of those HP42s going into service, Imperial Airways followed the same enterprising policy by ordering the even more modern Empire flying boat. This high-wing, four-engined aircraft still looks as aesthetically beautiful today as it did then. By 1937 the success of these 200 m.p.h. craft, needing no expensive runways (any open stretch of relatively sheltered water was sufficient) was assured. By 1938 Imperial Airways were operating 18 services a week with the 'Empire Boats' going to Egypt, India, East Africa, South Africa, Malaya and Australia. It was the advent of another war which stemmed such incredible frontier breaking. Experiments with transatlantic passenger services were being made and a mail service to America using mid air flight refuelling was actually operating when, for the second time, the lights went out all over Europe.

In 1939, resulting from the Cadman Committee findings a year earlier, the Civil Aviation Act went on the statutes. With the war drums having been rumbling since 1936 one can only assume that the Cadman Committee had been so intensely concentrating upon their findings that nothing else impinged upon their senses. British

Airways were given a clear licence to continue the European service, which they did up to 1940, and Imperial Airways were sternly rebuked for being 'too commercial'!

From the aftermath of war in 1945 however there was still a spark of that same spirit waiting to be rekindled. More than one ex RAF pilot plunged his gratuity, experience and faith into small commercial ventures with surplus wartime aircraft. One Air Vice Marshal, Donald Bennett of Pathfinder fame, using converted Lancasters and Yorks established the British South American Airways in March 1946, and back like Phoenix from the ashes came the Empire Flying Boats, for a brief re-run with BOAC. Nationalisation started in 1940 and continued in 1948, yet old divisions survived with BEA operating autonomously leaving BOAC to function as a separate company. This peculiar anomaly existed until the late sixties. There was a proliferation of government committees looking into everything in those years. The Edwards Committee sat in 1967 to determine upon a restructure of the commercial airline traffic in the UK Another war could have broken out by the time their findings were made known in May of 1969.

THE STATELY GIANTS OF IMPERIAL AIRWAYS
It's very debatable but I still incline to the argument that these were the very first custom built airliners to go into regular service. Others, such as the Armstrong Whitworth Ensign, were coming onto the scene but through the mid thirties the silver bodied HP42s certainly were the centre of attraction at Croydon Aerodrome. Celebrities who had previously been photographed by the press boarding the 'Golden Arrow' now courted publicity by boarding the Hercules or Hannibal for the morning flight to Paris, knowing that the *Tatler* or the *London Illustrated News* would have their cameramen at the ready.
Oil on canvas, 28" × 36"

Another two years of deliberation and in August 1971 the Civil Aviation Act came into being which set up the Civil Aviation Authority to replace the old Air Transport Licencing Board.

Following this a new British Airways Board was set up, but the jealous adherence to different titles was not really settled until 1974, when an effective merger was declared. Even then it was 1976 before the blanket coverage of British Airways really took effect. By this time there was an immense escalation of air traffic right across the world with London being the central hub for all international traffic. In 1979 British Airways made the bold but justifiable decision to adopt a policy of short term expansion and growth. That merger earlier on though had given them not only extra equipment and extra markets but extra problems. The doubling of forces had resulted in duplication of staff. Their declared objective of doubling growth dwindled away when there was also a doubling of costs. By 1980 the world economy was creating the situation that was affecting so many other large industries and British Airways was just another victim of international inflation and trade slumps. In the year 1980-81 BA was £145 million in the red, and in '81-82 showed a deficit of £545 million.

Sir John King, appointed chairman in 1981, still faced a long downhill run economically, but his tough realistic approach to the problems eventually saw them 'bottom out' in 1982 with that horrendous loss to start the long arduous climb up again in 1983.

The inherited problem of duplicated manpower was tackled head-on. There was no other way. A staff that had ballooned to an unwieldy 58,000 was severely pruned to 35,000. £400 million was just written off in the company's books. There was no alternative to that either. Gradually, the benefits started to show. The staff cuts showed a saving of hundreds of millions of pounds, (an efficient streamlined staff in 1986 still accounted for £722 million in costs) and having been at one time fully stretched to just pay the interest (£120 million) on their debts, the company was now able to start paying off the capital. There was a new light on the horizon, caution was still the order of the day, but the retrenchment period was over and the future looked to be promising once more a period of growth and expansion.

In 1952 BOAC had stunned the world with a sleek, beautiful aircraft supplied by de Havilland. The Comet was not only a magnificent record breaker, but the very first of a new generation of airliners. Frank Whittle's jet engines had successfully powered warplanes long before the Second World War had ended but no airline seemed anxious to take the first steps in commercial jet travel after 1945. Everyone had continued with the well tried piston engined aircraft until de Havilland, surprisingly enough with ministry backing, launched the Goblin jet engined Comet.

Britain lost its lead in jet aircraft design overnight thanks to the tragic demise of the Comet in 1952 and it looked unlikely that such a success could ever be repeated. But in 1976 the most ambitious project of the day came to fruition and the Anglo-French-built supersonic Concorde went into service. As exciting if not as beautiful as the Comet, the Concorde had no immediate rivals. On 21 January the great white bird flew from London to Bahrain, breaking all records. Along the English coast it became a popular pastime to record the sonic booms it left in its wake. But in New York in November the sonic booms were not so popular. Concorde had flown into the Federal Airport at Washington with no problem, but the borough of Queens in New York, indulging in local politics, brought repeated objections to the aircraft's landings, and it took a long time plus the UK Federal Courts to find a solution.

Concorde had been a government backed exercise, an exercise that had left them with a most imposing set of muscles in the air traffic business, but also a set of development costs that totalled £1200 million. British Airways were keen to operate such a record breaking aircraft, but no company anywhere on earth could take over a set of books with that debit figure in the columns.

An agreement was met whereby, broadly, British Airways took over the aircraft faced only with its operating costs, and the government absorbed those development costs already incurred. Even so, maintaining such an ultra modern piece of equipment was costly. There was opposition to it from New York, which at the time looked insuperable, and possible flights to India and Kuala Lumpur were not viable because of problems to do with territorial overflights.

Was this great bird flying 10 miles high at 1500mph going to become the veritable albatross? It may have looked like it to some, but if a product is that good it cannot be grounded forever. Critics may have dubbed it a white elephant but they were soon confounded. Concorde continued to fly, as graceful as any albatross, but too high and too fast ever to worry an ancient mariner. Her seats are now more sought after than any cut price fare and much more prestigious than any first class Jumbo ticket, and the number of entrepreneurial agents queuing up to book special charter flights increases daily. New York now welcomes Concorde's regular service flights and she is the *only* other transatlantic carrier that the prestigious *QEII* is proud to share her trip with.

I had assumed that today Concorde is something extra-special to BA and received appropriate treatment, but no – she is just another member of the fleet I was assured – though they did admit that her profits were substantial. Indeed, all of BA's profits are at long last substantial enough to enable their chairman, now Lord King, to taxi the company out to take-off point for public ownership.

In seven years such a turnaround in any company's fortunes can only be the result of intense dedication, first class management and above all enterprise.

THE BIG WHITE BIRD
This was the very first Concorde to fly. Now, exactly the same design but proudly wearing the uniform of BA, the big white bird leads the world in its much sought after, supersonic, prestige flights.
Watercolour, 22"×28"

The Cream of Cornish Industry

ENGLISH CHINA CLAYS

*I*n the early years of the sixteenth century Michelangelo chose the stone for his sculptures from the marble quarries of Carrara. In the twentieth century the Cornish firm of English China Clays also select their marble from the same source that supplied arguably the world's greatest sculptor with the superb, malleable stone from which he produced his commissions for the House of Medici. No *David* or *Pieta* will emanate though from St Austell in mid-Cornwall. ECC's marble is destined to improve the quality of paper, and like china clay is used as a coating pigment in the paper industry.

There is however one piece of superb craftmanship on display in the lobby of ECC's headquarters, John Keay House, that I'm sure Michelangelo would have passed with approval. It is a copy of Josiah Wedgwood's famous Portland vase – No.11 to be precise of a limited edition of twenty-five that the pottery firm produced for an anniversary year. Whilst the connection with Michaelangelo may be somewhat tenuous there *is* nonetheless a direct historical link.

In the early 1800s Wedgwood, in company with Spode and Minton and other Staffordshire potters, homed in on St Austell in a style not unlike that of the later Californian goldrush. That area of Cornwall had been proved to have the most productive concentrate of kaolinised granite (china clay) anywhere in Europe. It was in fact to become, a hundred and fifty years later, the biggest single concentrate of primary deposits* of china clay in the world. It gave the Staffordshire potters, hungry for quality products, the alchemy they all sought, a clay that was soft and malleable when worked, strong but not brittle when fired and, above all, with a purity of texture and whiteness of colour that had not been available to them before.

From 1746 William Cookworthy, a Quaker apothecary-cum-potter, had monopolised its extraction for many years. He had first come across rich kaolin deposits farther west in Cornwall at Tregonning Hill in Helston, home of the famous Furry Dance, before discovering the vast area of granite beneath the subsoil of the moors above St Austell. He must have had some geological knowhow our potting Quaker. Granite is one of the most common igneous rocks, particularly in Cornwall – but very few granites have been altered in the way the Cornish granite has, and it is this extra bonus thanks to the work of mother nature that produces the 'kaolinised' deposits better known as china clay. Mother nature started the hydro thermal process that supplied the foundations for

*Clay sited where it was originally formed.

OPENING A NEW MINE
Even in twenty years this is one
operation that has seen little change.
The 'crawlers' and excavators may
have got a little bigger but the scene
is so reminiscent of the very first
mine – Littlejohns – that I watched
being opened up in 1967.
Watercolour, 22" × 30"

ECC in the carboniferous age 300 million years ago, when St Austell
– indeed the whole of the British Isles – was under the sea. By the
time this little island had pulled itself out of the briny, the long
process of compression and eruption had done its job and 25 square
miles of southern Cornwall was waiting for a certain Quaker
apothecary to come along and discover its rich secret.

From there, via the marble quarries of Italy and the great
artist/sculptor Michelangelo, down the ages with the artists of the
pottery world, it was a long haul to 1967. That year a much humbler,
less vaunted artist visited the clay pits of ECLP as this great
company was known then. I had taken my sketchbook and painter's
observational powers, such as they are, along to St Austell at the
directors' invitation. I was impressed then. Twenty years later I was
doubly impressed. The expected increase in technology was well
evident. But conservation too, due to increasing pressure over the
last decade, now occupies considerable amounts of the company's
time and skills. It was, though, the vastly increased scale and the
diversity of ECC's operations that impressed me on this visit. They
could have been content to have continued as the operators of the

world's finest kaolin, simply fulfilling orders from customers worldwide. That operating base would have remained safe and permanent. But ECC chose not to. Instead they invested in a very sophisticated, highly technical sales campaign worldwide, side by side with an acquisitions policy. They sold themselves successfully as the best china clay suppliers in the world and at the same time acquired new bases and depots across the world: Atlanta, Texas, Singapore, Tokyo, Brussels, Helsinki, Milan, Paris, Dusseldorf and Gothenburg. In addition, thirty clay stores are spread throughout Europe, giving both strategic reserves and packaging and supply services.

At home, diversification has brought them into the quarrying and building industry. With materials supplied from their own network of UK-based quarries, they build houses from Cornwall to Kent. They are also into earth moving, civil engineering, waste disposal (they have *had* to become experts in that), and their mining activities embrace other minerals besides china clay with a total output of over 5 million tonnes of industrial minerals. But it is still the kaolin or china clay which claims most production time and most customers.

There is an annual total of 4.7 million tonnes of china clay produced in the whole of western Europe. Three million tonnes of that comes from the west country mines of ECC, 80 per cent of that output goes to the world's paper industry as fillers and coatings.

The original customers, the ceramics industry, take some 12 per cent of the clay annually from ECC. This includes 'ball clay', a

OPENING UP LITTLEJOHNS PIT, 1967
This was my first introduction to ECLP (as they were then known), twenty years ago. I watched fascinated as the giant dozers and crawlers carved out the great open bowl in the ground and the overburden was trucked away to add another white mountain to St Austell's skyline.

Today a new pit presents much the same scene and is dug out in much the same way. What has changed now though is the resiting of the waste or overburden.

No longer is it sufficient to add another peak to the local 'alps'. Nowadays escarpments, infilling and grass seeding allied to soil conservation and reforestation are part of the policy to try and usefully transform every seven tonnes of waste that is the cost of every single tonne of china clay extracted.
Oil on board, 36" × 48" (from the collection of Mrs. Hamilton Crotty).

secondary deposit* of kaolinized mineral, lacking the whiteness and purity of primary china clay but still in demand. Prehistoric man discovered the plasticity of ball clay and when the first potter's wheel spun ball clay was used. ECC's seams of ball clay in Devon and Dorset were first mined in pre-Roman days and later by the Romans themselves.

Though they may still be drawing upon 3,000-year-old sources of minerals, ECC are right in the front line when it comes to modern products. Their extensive research programme has taken them into other industrial minerals such as calcium carbonates. CA CO^3 has been around for a long time, chiefly in chalk, marble and limestone, but it was more recent and rapid developments in the plastics and paint industries that accelerated research into the use of calcium carbonates. At present this mineral product makes up only 20 per cent of their china clay output, but judging from the way ECC move I wouldn't take any bets on what the percentage might be in ten years' time.

Conservation

The 'white pyramids' of southern Cornwall have been around a long time now, some of them for 200 years. The subject of much debate and controversy, these great mountains of waste and overburden have been alternately praised by poets and blasted by politicians. Generations of inhabitants of the St Austell area accept them as part of the environment. One of the local pubs is named after them and when the industry is the biggest employer in the county you are not going to complain too much if the skyline looks more like a little Switzerland than the Cornish Riviera.

Nature has done her best with some of the older 'pyramids'. Natural seeding has taken place and flora indigenous to the area has given a cosmetic overlay in places. But with a great nutrient deficiency in the waste soils more was needed than just wind and rain could supply. With at least seven tonnes of waste material for every single tonne of marketable clay produced, the environmental problem is immense. Where site and working demands permit, overburden and waste are now bulldozed in long, low escarpments or embankments.

Collaboration between the ECC research department and boffins at Liverpool University's Department of Botany produced a technique of spraying steep slopes with a slurry mix that contained not only suitable seedlings but also nitrogen-bearing clovers which help build up the nutrient growth.

Local rivers which at one time ran white when clay production was at a high now flow their natural colour – and production is even higher. This spectrum pollution was caused by the unwanted mica, separated and discharged at the refining stage. ECC laid a network of some 15 miles of polyurethane piping to channel all the mica into lagoons or worked-out pits. There it dries out sufficiently for the area to be seeded in grass. Soay sheep have been introduced for

---

*Clay moved or washed away from the source where it was originally formed.

---

grazing and initial experiments in planting crops, potatoes, other vegetables and winter wheat have so far been quite successful.

Their own 10-hectare tree nursery suggests that ECC's conservation efforts are not just a cosmetic stopgap. Elsewhere in the country a large-scale forestation policy of conifers only causes concern on account of that species' heavy nitrogen consumption rate; ECC are researching a wide variety of hard and softwood trees. In May and June you will see glorious splashes of colour from masses of tree lupins. They add a beautiful touch to the landscape but they aren't there just as decoration, for this particular plant enriches the nitrogen in the soil, keeps down the weeds and provides shelter for all the young trees planted around them.

Drink your coffee from that nice pottery mug, beautify yourself with cosmetics, open up your glossy magazine, dip a brush into a paint pot or take some remedy for that poorly tummy: with all of these actions you will be taking advantage of the final products from that land of the white pyramids.

MICHELANGELO'S MARBLE QUARRY AT CARRARA
This quarry in northern Italy, forming a magnificent scene in its own right, once provided the marble for the famous sculptor. Michelangelo demanded the very best quality stone for his work and 500 years later the same quality is expected for china clay usage.
Watercolour, 25" × 17"

Down the Hatch and Round the Horn

WHITBREAD & CO

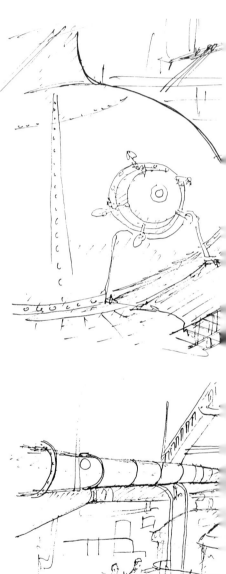

Whitbread's Porter Tun Room in Chiswell Street, deep in the City of London, has become well known in recent years for housing that modern equivalent of the Bayeux Tapestry, the Overlord Embroidery. Its splendid king post roof, next in size to Westminster Hall, is high on the index of architectural significance. A few years ago I was able to appreciate the beauties of both when Whitbread hosted an event for the Mary Rose Trust, another piece of history they helped sponsor. At that time I had no idea of the deeper history behind the place. Neither did I know that only a few years before, in 1976, Whitbread had still been brewing on the premises, the very last brewery to produce beer in the City of London. Few of the visitors on that occasion knew that the very elegant room that they occupied had once been flooded with the best of British porter, intentionally!

The story starts with Samuel Whitbread the first, born in 1720. Samuel was the seventh of eight children from a family of good English yeoman stock. How the choice of a brewer's training was made is not recorded but it cost his widowed mother £300 (a small fortune in those days) to apprentice young Samuel to the Brewers' Company in 1736. Whoever made the decision, it was a sound one. Young Whitbread learned well and he learned fast. He was only twenty–two when he set up in business with Godfrey and Thomas Shewell. Some twenty years later both his partners had retired from the business and Samuel was pursuing his own ideas of development and production. He had purchased earlier the little Kings Head Brewhouse in Chiswell Street, and this was to be the beginnings of the great Whitbread empire.

Ale had been brewed and drunk in this country for centuries, but by reason of its hit–or–miss methods of production the customer never really knew what he might be getting to quench his thirst before his first sip (or smell!). In those days if you were fairly flush you ordered a jug of 'strong' or 'twopenny' beer. The less well off could only afford halfpenny beer, which might well be designated by the landlord himself as 'stale' or 'cloudy'. The problem lay in finding a lasting preservative. The addition of hops alone had never been sufficient, until the arrival of porter. First brewed in Shoreditch, porter changed the whole scene. With the introduction of heavily roasted brown malt continually mashed, brewers now had a much greater degree of control over quality and storage, once an increasing hazard, was now easy and safe and furthermore increased maturity.

This opened the doors – or rather the brewery vats – to mass production. Samuel Whitbread, recognising the new benefits, sat up overnight watching the brewhouse copper in Chiswell brewery, like a devoted nurse watching over a sick child. But there was nothing sick about Whitbread's brew. It was one of the best. Popularity demanded greater production and Whitbread's answer was to use the porter vaults not to store the ale barrels but to fill the whole vaults with the brew. All he needed to do was to make the floor and walls waterproof, or rather beerproof – waterproofing might have been easier. Whitbread's best beer was anxious to get to its public and Smeaton's best cement wasn't going to stop it flowing through the walls. Robert Mylne, designer of Blackfriars Bridge, had been consulted to no effect, and Josiah Wedgwood and Company had been requested to make glazed tiles for the walls. This last was a sound enough idea one would think, considering how many jugs, mugs and servers the famous potters successfully put around all sorts of liquid, but they did not feel up to competing with Whitbread's best brew. It was finally a combination of shipwright caulking, metal plates and ties that stemmed the leaks in 1784.

Over forty-five years through sheer diligence and enthusiasm Samuel had also made his mark both socially and politically. In 1768 he became a whig MP, but in no way treated this simply as a reflection of worldly success, as so many did. The younger Samuel Whitbread did not share the same enthusiasm or instinct for the family business; he was far more inclined towards playing the part of an MP. He used his position at Westminster to espouse many just and worthy causes, not the least of which were the abolition of the slave trade and the introduction of the first minimum agricultural wage act into Parliament.

A devout churchgoer, he clung to basic religious principles as surely as he clung to his business ones. Never in his lifetime was the Sabbath allowed to be broken by himself, his family or anyone in the Whitbread employ. Probably the greatest if briefest testimony to Samuel Whitbread came from the Prince Regent upon his death in July 1815: 'The noblest work of God hath indeed perished – he was an honest man'. From a man who constantly saw hypocrisy and sycophancy at its most developed it was indeed a great compliment.

With the elder Samuel devoting more time to parliamentary affairs over the last few years of his life the business, from having produced 200,000 barrels yearly up to 1800, began to fall and in 1810 dropped to 111,000. Three years before the founder's death merger with Martineau & Bland brought in new blood, and there has been a Martineau as a director ever since. They have had a great and beneficial influence on the company but the porter they helped brew became too much for one of the early partners: in 1834 John Martineau, overcome by either the fumes or apoplexy, was discovered dead, having fallen into the vat.

Another partner, Shaw Lefevre, who became Speaker of the House of Commons in 1840, started off the tradition of Whitbread providing the horses for the Speaker's coach. Later Whitbread family stock though was to reinforce the company again and by the end of the nineteenth century the old drive and business flair had

returned to revitalise the business. The widescale production of bottled beer also helped the fortunes of Whitbread.

There are many fascinating and significant episodes in Whitbread's history that, sadly, we cannot record here, and we have to bridge the company's progress over a period of two world wars to come to 1945 with Colonel W. H. Whitbread chairing the board. The company had undergone drastic changes through that period, as indeed had the whole of the brewing industry. The costs of large-scale bottling and distribution were such that few small breweries could remain in the market. From 1945 to 1970 the number of independent brewers fell from 703 to 177. Whitbread was not a small company but neither was it a giant. Colonel Whitbread, reading the signs early, put forward a policy of expansion which led to company shares going on the public market for the first time in 1948.

Mackeson's Stout, acquired in 1929 and gaining popularity yearly, was the spearhead of a nationwide advertising campaign which featured the first ever 'commercial' on British television. From then on up to 1961 Mackeson's sales quadrupled. The power of impact advertising coupled with a good product showed the way to the rest of industry.

Fighting the Southern Ocean in the last Round the World Yacht Race
Watercolour, 22"×30"

In the fifties and sixties Whitbread may have appeared to have buttressed their expansion by swallowing up the minnows of the business. Not so. The small fry thankfully sought refuge under what became known as the 'Whitbread umbrella', a scheme put up by Colonel Whitbread and his board. The threatened company, instead of having to surrender total control to unwelcome outsiders, was able still to continue in business with Whitbread taking a small holding (25–35 per cent) and the company under siege having the benefits of Whitbread's technical and marketing advice. Such a benevolent association inevitably led to a desire for closer business contact and within ten years twenty such companies became Whitbread subsidiaries.

Samuel Whitbread the first would be a proud man could he see the state of his company today. Still a Samuel Whitbread leads the company, and the tremendous growth from 1945 to 1976 has seen their assets leap from £9,084,000 to £438,160,000, with their trade expanding right across the world. In 1987 their turnover worldwide was £1,553,900 million showing a profit of £158.9 million. Whitbread today is no longer just a British brewer. It is an international company producing and marketing all types of drinks from beers, wines and spirits to soft drinks. It is equally committed to the retailing of drinks and food through businesses such as Beefeater, Pizza Hut and Threshers. That historic link, the premises at Chiswell Street, will hopefully remain, and there are even longer links with the past through those splendid shire horses which can still be seen working daily around the City as well as on state occasions. Their lineage runs back to the great chargers that bore Henry V and his armoured knights to Agincourt.

One cannot leave Whitbread without some mention of the widespread sponsorship they give to sport. Colonel Whitbread himself once rode in the Grand National and with the company's long commitment to horse transport it is not surprising that this patronage has extended to the turf. The Whitbread Gold Cup is one of steeplechasing's classics and the Whitbread Trophy the holy grail of every three–day eventer at the Whitbread Badminton Horse Trials. However, the most dramatic, demanding and extended sporting event of all time must surely be the Whitbread Round the World Race. Started in 1973, it is an endurance test of 32,000 miles. The fifth race will start from the Solent in September 1989 and will take competitors to Uruguay before they head to Western Australia and on to New Zealand. From there the race runs round the dreaded Cape Horn and back to Uruguay. It is then a sprint to the Florida sailing resort of Fort Lauderdale. Last comes the Atlantic passage back home to Portsmouth. It is a race that demands everything from its participants and is indeed such a feat of physical endurance as well as intensive organisation that it can only be held every four years. It has become the premier event in sailing, involving sailors from nearly every country in the world. In the middle of all the glamour, excitement and drama enjoyed at the start down at Portsmouth, the sight of packs of pale ale being stowed away with yacht stores reminds us who the sailing world have to thank for this marathon sporting epic – Whitbread.

Britain's Invisible Asset

BRITISH GAS

When the product of a company cannot be seen or heard, such a product might suggest an illusory company. British Gas however is a most down-to-earth and industrious company.

Quite a large proportion of the nation's cooking and heating (and even lighting at one time) was provided by manufactured coal gas only twenty-five years ago. Then the gas industry was at the start of a revolution, changing from coal to oil and imported natural gas for gas production. Then in the mid sixties oil companies searching in the North Sea found natural gas, and the industry was revolutionised again. Companies such as BP, Amoco, Philips, Shell and Total all developed methane-producing fields in the seas around our coastline and British Gas, itself a partner with Amoco in two of the biggest fields, was more than pleased to buy the gas from them.

As supplies multiplied the company was able to begin shedding old, capital- and labour-intensive production plants. Their sites had for years been tawdry and grim spectacles all over the country. There is a generation in Britain now though to whom that familiar old term 'the gasworks' will mean nothing. The black pyramids of coke and coal surrounding them often meant accompanying rail tracks and shunting goods wagons. For the very virtue that it needed its own supply of gas, no reasonably sized town seemed to be free of this particular backcloth to its local landscape. And by golly you could *smell* the company product in those days! Though you might have difficulty in finding the railway station in a strange town the local gasworks usually presented no difficulty. When the breakthrough to natural gas came its most beneficial effect was at the time not fully appreciated. But surely in ridding our towns and cities of the nineteenth-century gasworks it gave us all the most splendid conservation bonus we could wish for?

As the supply of natural gas was increased and the last of the gasworks made redundant, so a new delivery system started. Now a nationwide pipeline system, forming a 'gas grid', moves the gas from its various shore terminals. This national transmission system, begun in 1964, is now 3,300 miles long – with all the subsidiary systems Britain's gas supply system now totals 145,000 miles. Or, if you want the old 'laid end to end' comparison, it means the pipework could be wrapped around mother earth five times and still have enough left over to tie a secure knot. And it is all buried underground, like the product, unseen and unheard.

We do not have the ugly old gas production plants any longer but many of the traditional gas holders have been kept, suitably sited, to give a back-up reserve to the local main system. They are filled of course with methane gas at low pressure. At very low temperatures natural gas liquefies and occupies much less space, Hence we have LNG (liquefied natural gas) storage to help meet winter demand for gas. Other special methods have been devised for storage of natural gas. Perhaps the most intriguing of these – if not unique, being a partially depleted offshore gasfield – is the Rough Field which has been cleverly engineered to become a vast storage reservoir. With the constant supply through a continuous grid feed pushing the gas along at up to 1000 pounds per square inch, one may wonder why we still need to resort to storage. It is of course the siting of our island home that is responsible. Up in our corner of the northern hemisphere the weather makes it essential to be prepared for exceptional unexpected demands. The majority of gas is used for heating. Extreme temperature changes cause variations in demand from one part of the country to another and from hour to hour. Back-up reserves linked to the grid are the answer.

British Gas has contracts with more than sixty different companies for the purchase of natural gas, often over a time span of twenty years and more. One year's purchase of supply can amount to more than £3000 million, so you have to have a pretty wide customer field when that sort of cost is involved. British Gas has just on *17 million* customers all told. When that many are using the product, the production figures begin to make sense. And that 17 million are specifically *customers*, those who pay the bills. As many of them are large firms in industry and catering, not to mention 16½ million households, one is talking of many more than 17 million people using gas.

British Gas is determined to be not only a customer to the gas producers, but a producer itself. In 1974 it had a rich find in Morecambe Bay which it proceeded to develop as another 'reserve' production unit that can feed in supplies to the grid for peak demands at short notice. This field was totally the result of their own exploration and its platforms are British Gas's own design. An unorthodox 'on the slant' drilling method has been devised here to ensure maximum output from the minimum number of platforms. These installations are designed to have a working life of forty years – and the cost of setting up ran into hundreds of millions of pounds.

Talk of thousands of miles of pipelines and reserve storage systems would seem to indicate that customers' gas is there waiting when they want it. Customarily it is, but it isn't quite so simple for the suppliers. Computerised control systems have had to be developed to enable the national and regional control centres to monitor and adequately and economically to supply the various and differing demands. National controllers with computerised weather forecasts and demand analyses advise them, and they make decisions based upon demands from the regions. A buyer from a big retail chain might feel responsible if he has a budget of hundreds of thousands of pounds. A British Gas national controller is basically a buyer too – but his budget runs into *millions* of

pounds. From twenty-six different North Sea fields the national controllers can write cheques or at least authorisation accounts for more than £30 million in one day. In the regions, electronic pressure and flow meters indicate to their officers how demand is being met. The customer must be satisfied and at the same time the national controllers do not want to buy more than is needed. They have their back-up stocks for emergency but there is no profit in laying up 'gas mountains'.

Nearly 60 per cent of the energy provided to private homes is gas, mostly for heating and hot water, which means more than 16 million domestic users. This means a customer increase in ten years of more than 25 per cent. Thirty-three per cent of the energy demand from the commercial users – offices, hotels, schools, restaurants and such like – is met by British Gas and a third of all gas sold went to industry, to supply nearly 40 per cent of the country's industrial heating.

Research and Development

Although their product is destined entirely for the home market, British Gas expertise is sold to more than twenty overseas countries, including the United States, Japan, China, and Western Germany. Research and development over the years has resulted in a separate division now employing some 2,000 people. This largely consists of engineering and science graduates who have advanced the technology and efficiency of not only finding and producing gas but of its transportation and use. An annual investment of around £70 million for this division has more than paid off. From it has sprung International Consultancy Services, literally engaged in selling British Gas know-how to foreign companies.

The most significant achievement on British Gas's business success score sheet is surely the fact that this year it 'went public'. The British public en masse may be strangers to the intricacies of the world of the stock market but they know a good thing when they see it and the response to the invited share issue was overwhelming. British Gas know-how may be going overseas, but the British were determined that their profits should stay at home.

Gas platform in Morecambe Bay
Acrylic, 15" × 22"

Printers' Suppliers Par Excellence

HOWSON-ALGRAPHY

It seemed that my itinerary had suddenly gone into reverse when I walked onto a factory floor in North Yorkshire. I was at Seacroft, near Leeds, but could well have been near the North Wales border at Shotton steel works judging by the scene before my eyes: a huge, long factory, with row upon row of coils of shining steel. Overhead swung the great gantry crane which moved the rolls of metal from one place to another.

But this wasn't British Steel at Shotton and neither were those gleaming metal rolls of steel. They were aluminium, and the factory was that of the biggest printing plate suppliers in the country. The aluminium is used in 100 per cent of their total output, for the production of printing plates mainly for the newspaper industry all over the world. At home, just about half of Fleet Street uses Howson-Algraphy plates, and there are another thousand news media customers spread across the globe.

Howson-Algraphy is a company with a multi-million pound turnover and, though now a part of the Vickers corporate group, still operates as a self-financing private company and claims in fact to be the biggest profit maker in the group. Like many big companies, however, they had small beginnings. Back in 1898 on the famous 'Printers Mile' in London's Tudor Street, Algraphy (no Howson then) had foreseen the potential of aluminium lithographic printing plates. Taking up a series of patents, Algraphy had expanded successfully as both manufacturer and supplier, moving to bigger premises over the years and finally arriving at Peckham in 1937. The supply of anodised aluminium plates strengthened their business and by 1960 they had branches in Leeds, Birmingham and Bristol.

1963 saw them widening their scope with the production of specialised printing chemicals, using a new plant in Margate. This was a major development, opening up as it did a completely new market to them and to their existing customers while still broadly remaining the same business.

But there was another producer in the same line of business: Hector Howson. He had been aware of an unsatisfied market demand for printing chemicals. It is surprising that as recently as then printers had relied upon their own amateur laboratory efforts to produce lacquers, coatings and wash up liquids. Consequently there was rarely a constant standard. Most reliance was placed upon the printing plate itself and the equally important back-up services were prey to trial and error. Hector's new company, set up in 1943, W. H. Howson, forged an important link in this chain of services and through the forties and fifties became the only serious competitor to Algraphy.

When Howson also produced an anodised aluminium printing plate and, like their competitors, moved to larger premises, it began to look like a major market clash or a compromise. But when in 1957 Howson's moved to the Mint building in Holbeck, Leeds, it wasn't Algraphy who joined forces with them – it was R. W. Crabtree, who had taken over Howson earlier that same year. In 1965 Vickers acquired Crabtree, not fully realising at the time that a potentially very important part of the Crabtree organisation was a relatively small printers' supply company. Four years later, in 1971, the acquisition of Algraphy by Vickers was a shrewd, if logical, move to achieve within their group the union of the two specialist firms which was to become one of the most successful printers' suppliers in the world.

Howson-Algraphy: it's something of a tongue twister isn't it? Do what everyone does to make it easy: substitute the vowel 'a' – or 'o' if you prefer – for the syllable 'al'. The name Hos'nagraphy' is known and understood anywhere in the world where there's a printing machine, small or large.

Anywhere in the world? Yes, indeed. Its subsidiaries are established in Australia, Canada, France, Germany, Holland, Italy (from 1963), Portugal, Spain, Sweden and – a real measure of both their technical and marketing skills this – the United States. They have five main centres spread across the States, covering production and sales.

Back home, 32,500 square metres of factory space at Seacroft is impressive. Although, after the shock of finding what at first sight seemed to be a cold steel production plant, I was prepared for (if not anticipating) the various highly sophisticated departments: analytical chemistry department; research and development; technical department; quality control; despatch and stocking. For any modern competitive company their level of efficiency is outstanding.

Down in Norfolk they have another factory, nearly one third the size of Seacroft, where they produce 'pre-press' equipment, items such as printing down frames and plate processors. In 1982 the company, expert in the use of their own computers, launched a computer service to their customers.

It is the company's versatility which impresses, as much as their product and financial achievements. To me it always seems remarkable that in a company started by a single competitive entrepreneurial character, his spirit can survive and the quality he inspired continue. Long after any family genes have vanished the drive and enterprise that so often belonged to one individual can somehow thrive, change of name and environment notwith-standing.

This fact evidenced itself recently when, concerned that their press room chemicals sales were not keeping up such a high sales graph as they desired, a new presentation was decided upon. Overnight, a new packaging and a new name came into being. This was 'Profit Plus', initially introduced to printers in a package of six

bottles containing all the liquids needed for the working printer in a handy carrypack, now a favourite with all their customers. A straightforward marketing exercise you might say, but one significantly well thought out. Six different print liquids sold together. The quantity is exactly right, portability is ideal and the printer has his washouts, cleaners, solvents and etchers all together in the same pack. Easily handled, stored and checked.

Where I can, I try to thread any historical and ecological links through my accounts of various industries. There is the ingenious architecture and the extremely clever siting of the Seacroft factory (so clever that I drove right past it on the first approach!) but the most pleasing sign of caring comes not on the official tour of the factory site at all. Afterwards I spied a small sheltered lake in the factory's tree-lined grounds. When I walked around it there I saw a crude but effective hand-lettered notice sited prominently on its bank: 'Keep off. Ducks hatching'. The ducks were a family of mallards and somehow nature had got the message through to them that here in the middle of the country's biggest printing plate manufacturers they would be safe – and they were.

I had thought I was at Shotton steel works when I first walked into the Seacroft factory. Seeing this, and remembering the 'tern rafts' on Shotton's lake, I sensed a greater and more meaningful similarity between the two places.

Not another steel mill but aluminium printing plates being processed at Howson-Algraphy's factory near Leeds. *Watercolour and acrylic, 15"x22"*

An Industry of the Utmost Refinement

BRITISH PETROLEUM

*I*n any account of enterprising and successful companies in British industry it is inevitable that some pretty big ones, even multinationals, are going to be included – and they don't come a lot bigger than BP. But it is not easy to distil a company such as this into a chapter. Their activities are so widespread that it is difficult to know where to start.

I first met them, as a corporate entity and as individuals, more than twelve years ago when I was invited to observe the setting up of their 'Forties' oil production platforms, and then later had the unforgettable experience of following the construction of the 800-mile pipeline that took the oil from its frozen wells 300 miles inside the Arctic Circle across the Jack London landscape of Alaska down to Valdez (the nearest deep water terminal that did not freeze over for ten months of the year). BP impressed me – then and now – as a company with tremendous driving force and yet with a great sense of responsibility and a workforce who, as individuals, were second to none at their jobs. If I were asked to put my finger on one particular pulse, it would be that of time. It may be too simplistic an observation, but one overriding factor I encountered everywhere was the awareness of the value of time. It was not obsessive, but whatever was being discussed or planned – major production, marketing, promotion, research, conservation, sponsorship – the overriding questions were 'When can we start?' and 'How long will it take?', with always the underlying inference, 'let's not waste time'. One can point a critical finger at many large corporations over waste in general terms, but you would have a job convincing BP of knowingly wasting that most precious of all commodities – time.

And if I were still pressed for another observation then it would be upon people: the characters, the men and women who run the company and who work for BP.

My visits to BP in 1987 were not as investigative or as extended as my experiences with them over the period from 1976 to 1978. But any changes wrought in the ten years since have been caused mainly by technological and marketing forces. Chairmen, divisional managers and directors have changed but a general character assessment if taken would remain the same. In any event, BP, like any observant and sensible company, is appreciative of talent and ability. Many of the men I met those years ago, men then in production jobs and junior management posts, have since won justified promotion.

When I first walked through the doors at Britannic House to be vetted (for such it was, however courteously done) Sir Eric Drake was just relinquishing the reins to the incoming chairman, David (later Sir David) Steel, since succeeded by Sir Peter Walters. The executive I first met was a tall, urbane and very tough public school/Army product called John Collins. John was the epitome of that character to whom Kipling addressed the lines:

'If you can keep your head when all about you
Are losing theirs and blaming it on you'

and 'If you can ... walk with Kings – nor lose the common touch.' John could, and had indeed, walked with kings, yet his common touch was always on call. His easy transition from a Buckingham Palace meeting, with all its attendant protocol, to an early and enjoyable get together with a hard boiled working crew on the drilling platform of a North Sea oil rig, was an education to watch.

After the Army John learned the oil business the hardest of hard ways, out in Saudi Arabia. Roughneck, roustabout, production supervisor: you name it, he had done it. I never was quite sure of his job title through all the time I knew him. Certainly he had a roving commission and seemed to head up the entire PR department for BP, but if he had the ear and the trust of the chairman (which he did) he did not use that as a crutch. He did things *his* way, but his way was, in his devout opinion, the way BP should be doing it.

He was not often wrong, though I suspect when he was he was quite unrepentant. It was through John Collins during my visits to Aberdeen and BP's offshore operations that I met a soulmate of his, Matt Linning. They had served a lot of their BP time together and in doing so forged a deep and lasting friendship. The pair of them shared the same qualities of toughness, resourcefulness and leadership, and yet were two quite different characters. Collins was forceful, but could wear down opposition with persistance, a smooth aggression was overlaid with remarkable charm. Linning was more quicksilver. His rich, constructive ideas were constantly bubbling to the surface and he wanted everyone to act upon them immediately. Like many BP men he lived life at a cracking pace. The 'work hard, play hard' policy could have been instituted by him, though one has to say that the playing occupied far less time than the working. When I first met him the Press had just given him the title 'Mr Forties'.

Matt Linning's correct title in BP then was I believe 'General Manager BP Forties Exploration', but for once the media had come up with a near acronym that was totally fitting. There were a lot of things without which the Forties Field would have had severe problems, but there is no doubt in the mind of anyone who was there in those early days that without the forceful drive and constant dedication of 'Mr Forties' that particular oil field would never have been completed on time nor be operating with the same degree of success. When I went up to Aberdeen the first time it wasn't sufficient that my presence had been okayed by BP's chairman: I had to satisfy 'Mr Forties' that I passed *his* bill of requirements. Fortunately I did, and in doing so formed a valued if brief friendship with the man. Matt's enthusiasms extended in all directions. I had known him for some time when he suddenly discovered that I had never made a parachute jump. I foolishly remarked that in retrospect I half regretted that it had never quite happened. Matt

NORTH SEA PRODUCTION PLATFORM
For me an offshore oil (or gas) platform is still the most dramatic example of man's constructive technology mastering nature. Mastering nature? Well, reaching a compromise with it anyway in inserting a tubular steel frame into the sea bed that will allow the sea to assail it and crash through it without actually wrecking it while at the same time man continues to pump up precious oil and gases from Neptune's storehouse. Standing on the drilling deck in the middle of a force eight gale one can easily – or rather, *uneasily* – assume that nature has forgotten all about that compromise and is going to show you just how little man's superiority means to her! *Watercolour and acrylic, 22" × 15"*

Enterprise on Canvas

was delighted. 'We'll do one together', he announced. 'We'll do a sea drop right by Forties Bravo – it will make marvellous publicity.' Matt would have made it happen all right. Fortunately at that moment we were each of us bound for widely separated destinations. I had word through a mutual friend more than a year later that he had not forgotten about 'the jump' and as soon as we could get together again ...

Matt could convincingly inculcate madcap ideas in one, and even shared enthusiasm, but in his absence I have to admit I did not pursue the jump too hard. Yet, I now have regrets. 'Mr Forties' left the Forties and us forever in 1987 and we shall now never make that crazy jump together.

Matt Linning would have been in his element in Alaska. In that environment one just has to accept such melodramatic phrases as 'dealing with primitive forces' and 'confronted by nature in the raw'. Melodramatic-sounding maybe, but true – totally true. It was another 'character' from BP who personally introduced me to and travelled around with me in that field of operations. Dr Jack Birks (then Director of Exploration and Production) and I had first met in 1975 and he with typical grace introduced me to all we met as a friend rather than a BP sponsored artist! Such warm informality enabled me to savour and appreciate the whole scene much more quickly than might otherwise have been the case. Jack Birks was tough enough too, but the toughness was never on show. He came over as a gentle and modest man, but as a mining engineer he had few peers. Certainly his top American counterparts (in whom modesty was a rare quality) afforded him great respect. 'Gee, your Doctor Birks sure knows what he's about', one remarked to me with a deference that amounted to awe.

But then, I haven't met a BP man who doesn't know what he's about. From divers to drilling engineers, from roustabouts to research chemists, they certainly know their jobs. Theirs is an industry that demands efficiency and those demands seem to mould a certain class of man. Characters, personalities, natures, do of course all differ, but one thing they all seem to share is the absorption with the end product of their particular job, be it production, research, servicing or whatever. Satisfaction does not seem to revolve entirely around the weekend off and the monthly pay cheque.

When I travelled up to Grangemouth to BP's only UK crude oil refinery, the scene was so different from offshore operations around the coast and a far far cry from any overseas exploration or development plant that I had not anticipated that same distinctive quality of job pride. Any platform or ship offshore can adopt a dramatic, or even romantic, guise. In the Middle East the exotic environment can cloak the everyday routine and present-day strife out there certainly adds drama. But in Grangemouth you have none of these desirable or heroic embellishments, there you just have acres and acres of steel pipes, storage vaults and towers. I was driven past row upon row of plants that all looked identical and yet were doing different operations. Towering columns of steel, steel pipes, steel chimneys, steel storage tanks, steel frames and steel ladders reminded me of that old Chaplin film *Modern Times,* with its backdrop scenery mirrored a hundred times. But hot steam escaping, stealing out into the cold and damp November atmosphere, created its own local cloud base and any *Modern Times* magic was soon lost in the turgid mist wrapping itself around everything.

The working environment at Grangemouth certainly wouldn't encourage over-romantic ideas of job satisfaction. But when Ron Finlay had first met me and started giving me a conducted tour of Scotland's only major oil refinery, sombre visual images formed no part of his outlook: Ron saw it strictly as a working unit of highly productive efficiency. Once more my meeting with a BP man was made easy because of mutual friends within the business. A lifetime in BP had given him direct and intimate knowledge of anyone whom I had chanced to meet in my relatively short acquaintance with the company, whether they were directors or field workers. Brief mention of the zany humour of one particular drilling rig worker I had met on my travels elicited an instant chuckle of recognition from Finlay. 'That would be old Algy' he said, and proceeded to add yet more to that particular character's personal history.

So, Ron Finlay was in charge of public relations at Grangemouth and as such was duty bound to ensure that any observer was given the best impressions. But thirty odd years of service had not noticeably dented his pride in BP. Neither did he attempt to hide anything. In the worst weather and some 600 miles from my own fair Cornish home, the refinery struck me as a nightmarish complex of pipework, tanks, steam and oil, but to Finlay and the men he introduced me to, this environment was quite normal. Their only concern with it was that it should function, and function well. The incoming flow of 'crude' from offshore must not be interrupted and the resultant outgoing of refined oil should be interrupted only if, for some reason, it were not of the desired quality.

Until 1919 the oil industry in Scotland had been dependent upon shale oil. Dr James 'Paraffin' Young pioneered a system of refining shale oil in the mid nineteenth century which laid the foundation for the same basic techniques that are used today. Australian, South African, Iranian and the Gulf oil refineries all owe their expertise to those shale oil technicians who travelled worldwide to help set up those early industries.

Somewhere in my early encounters with oilmen I heard a tale about some forgotten minor diplomat in Persia in the early 1900s who, so the story went, kicked an obstinate camel (presumably without much effect), then vented his anger on kicking dried cakes of camel dung that lay on the dry sandy surface. It dawned on the touchy diplomat that this was a strange dropping to come from a camel – or from any quadruped for that matter. These sand-covered pancakes proved to be not dung of any description, but congealed cakes of oil – oil forced to the surface by the intense heat and by the abundant pressure of the oil well somewhere below.

Like many another, that tale is probably apocryphal. The brief sheet issued by BP merely states that William Knox d'Arcy was granted an oil concession by the Persian government in 1901. It would be intriguing to imagine the said Knox d'Arcy starting off such a mammoth enterprise because he became disgruntled with a camel. If he did, the camel was at a place called Masjid-i-Suleiman, because it was there in 1908 that the first commercial oil discovery in the Middle East was made! The Anglo Persian Oil Company was founded the following year. That activity, plus the formation of their own tanker company, probably explains why it was another eighteen years before they took an interest in the Scottish shale oil industry. Perhaps they had been sufficiently impressed by the shale oil experts from Lothian who had advised them on setting up the Middle East refineries. Whatever the reason, the forerunners of BP acquired Scottish Oils Limited in 1919, and Grangemouth Museum has a very interesting section dealing with that early shale oil industry and its connections through to the present-day BP activities. There is no mention in their museum of any camels but it is intriguing to think of the Anglo *Persian* Oil Company taking over a traditional Scottish industry in 1919.

These two totally different fields of activity ten thousand miles apart gave little sign then of the important roles they were going to play in the world's oil markets seventy years later. Dr. James 'Paraffin' Young, William Knox d'Arcy and an unknown camel may seem a strange triumvirate but try and weave a more enthralling story around them than the one that exists!

The Big Cat

JAGUAR CARS

Many people know of the Jaguar history – know the glamorous Swallow bodies were put on production model chassis, bringing style and bright colours within reach of the many, how the low-slung SS1 was born in 1931 in the depth of the Great Depression and how its successor, the sensational 2½ litre, burst upon a startled world at the 1935 Olympia Show to set the pace for a series of designs. The dramatic merger with BMC in 1966 (re-named British Leyland in 1968) with the support of the great Sir William Lyons, followed by its independence once again under Sir John Egan and the recent resurgence of this proud marque – all are well known.

What Lord Montagu focuses on in his brilliant book *Jaguar* (which has been extensively quoted here) is what happened last year – for the company, which relied so heavily on one model, had a problem. How, and when, do you follow a model that is still enjoying considerable success? For a large manufacturer a poorly received new car would be a calamity. For Jaguar it would be a disaster. For this reason Jaguar management decided the new model must be evolutionary rather than revolutionary.

Whilst no item, other than the steering wheel badge, was interchangeable between the old and new models, nevertheless the designers decided to plump for gradually updating the concept rather than striving for a quantum leap. It was, in fact, a policy learnt from their German competitors.

In spite of this conservative policy, some £100 million had been expended on development with another £30 million or so swallowed by the new engines. These were offered in the new XJ6 in both 2.9 and 3.6 litre versions. At the time the plans were laid down for the car, economy was the first priority and no-one could imagine then that anyone would have any desire to purchase a V12 engined car by the mid-eighties. Hence the new body was designed merely to take the new family of engines. However, when Jaguar learnt that both their main rivals, BMW and Mercedes Benz, were working on such an engine, a re-think was necessitated. Jaguar could hardly allow their competitors to gain the extra prestige that such an engine engenders, unchallenged. Re-engineering the car to take the V12 unit was no easy task and dictated that the 'old' Series III must continue in V12 form for several years.

Whilst retaining traditional Jaguar values the new car was designed to be a step forward in terms of reliability and quality of manufacture. It was said to be 20 per cent easier to build, including

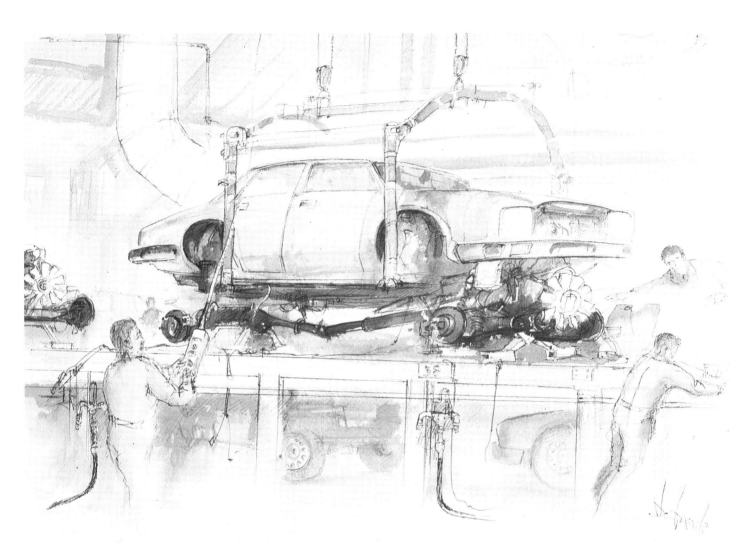

Jaguar: the assembly line
Acrylic and watercolour, 15" × 22"

the higher level of specification, and so productivity would be improved.

In the early eighties an Achilles heel of the Jaguar had been its electrical system, so that was a subject that received a considerable amount of development with the adoption of solid state circuitry in places.

Interestingly, Jaguar state that the new XJ6 is intended to be the first of a family of cars. There are ideas and firm plans for the current range (the AJ6-engined Jaguar XJ6, Jaguar Sovereign and Daimler) to grow.

Several problems had to be overcome to meet new productivity and quality requirements; the original XJ concept was a difficult act to follow. However, with so much at stake for the company, Jaguar have taken few risks and confidently believe, under the shrewd stewardship of Sir John Egan, that the car is a little better in every department. Acceleration, fuel consumption, interior noise levels are all a little improved. The body is smoother and prettier and the interior more elegant. It is widely rumoured that by the end of the decade the V12 engine will be available in a slightly stretched version and this will be needed to compete – especially with Mercedes Benz and BMW in Germany.

Whilst vehicle design and development had been receiving so much time, effort and expenditure during the early eighties, company development did not lag. Jaguar had inherited some less than satisfactory dealerships from the BL era – garages that were multi-franchise outlets, or to put it another way, garages which sold Minis, Land Rovers, Maestros and Jaguars alongside each other. This, Jaguar decided, was hardly the way to market an exclusive high class product.

Consequently a tough policy of weeding out these dealers and, wherever possible, setting up 'solus' dealers (that is, dedicated solely to Jaguar) took place. Thus when the new XJ6 was finally announced there was a sufficiently professional body of dealers able to do justice to the product, in terms of selling and servicing. Large sums were also invested in manufacturing to modernise the archaic plants and, whilst retaining traditional craftsmanship wherever necessary, adopt such modern aids as robotics to improve quality, consistency and productivity. A tremendous amount of effort was put into launching the new saloons before they were finally unveiled to the public at the 1986 Birmingham Motor Show. Previews, with much use of videos and dramatic effects, were given to groups of press, dealers from all over the world, union leaders, City luminaries and, interestingly and sensibly, the workforce which once again had pride in its company.

The press reaction was very favourable with many experienced journalists claiming that here was the finest car in the world, bar none. In many areas it was felt that the new Jaguars outshone their traditional rivals.

The car's agility and lighter feel were widely praised. With excellent road-holding and lively performance from the 3.6 litre, the new XJ6 was commended for being a more sporting car than its predecessor. The 2.9 litre engine, inevitably, did not sparkle in quite the same way in what was still a heavy car, as the engineers had found that it was not possible to retain traditional refinement without a certain weight penalty.

A very few bemoaned the rather conservative shape, suggesting that it would quickly become outdated and that Jaguar should have taken a bolder step forward, but most felt that it was a most sensible and stylish compromise.

Whatever, the public were not slow to record their approval and the orders flooded in putting Jaguar's new manufacturing set-up under great pressure as they grappled with the enviable problem. Within weeks the waiting list became more than a year in length, even before the US launch in May, 1987.

Production for 1986 was another record at 41,437 up 8 per cent on the previous year, and included 4,000 of the new cars. With the launch costs to absorb, profit was little changed at £120 million.

Following worldwide sales of 8,820 in 1986, the XJ-S range was improved and expanded from February the following year. The engine management technology developed for the XJ6 range was adopted on the 3.6 litre 'S' models and automatic transmission became an option.

Truly a story of British success.

The Pinnacle of Finance

NATIONAL WESTMINSTER BANK

We ordinary individuals accept the fact that a great deal of our working – and indeed, our leisure – lives are controlled by our relationship with the bank. Whether it be wages, savings, borrowings, investment or mortgages, we need the services of our High Street bank to operate them all efficiently. Industry is in exactly the same boat – the only difference being in the size of the sums involved. NatWest, as we call them, get involved in a lot of those massive sums on behalf of industry and are worth a visit, however brief.

Banking through the eighteenth and nineteenth centuries had evolved a not-so-subtle monopoly that forbade any bank having more than six partners – other than the Bank of England – to issue its own notes. At a time when notes issued upon a bank had little in common with the bank currency of today this ensured that banking was kept in the control of small local partnerships. There are many such small banking companies on the family tree of the National Westminster Bank of today. One of the most direct lines of descent goes back to the highly respectable Manchester & Liverpool District Banking Company, later to become well known as the District Bank. By 1834, having opened an account with the Bank of England, a prodigious and prestigious step in those days, the 'District' was a substantial concern indeed.

With the coming of the 1914-18 war, as with the Second World War, banking was threatened not only by enemy action but by erosion of its staff. In 1914 and 1915 the bank had to maintain a reserved occupation policy which was not helped when the Lord Mayor of London made an appeal for enlistment in the 'Bankers' Battallion'; 78 of the 'District's', 440 of National Provincial's staff and 505 of Westminster's gave their lives on the fields of Flanders. The second bloody maelstrom accounted for over 600 of the bank's strength, many of them in RAF service.

The immediate postwar years, as with industry generally, were a period of rebuilding and reappraisal. The new postwar age though was bringing sweeping changes to the financial and social structures of the country. Where once a bank account had been the prerogative of trade, the learned professions and the wealthy, it was now becoming a common facility for the man in the street. Firms started paying wages by cheque and the weekly wage earner as well as the salaried realised the benefits of High Street banking. The number of branches increased accordingly. By the middle sixties the Westminster Bank boasted 1,400 branches and between the

District Bank and the National Provincial, soon to become their partners, another 2,200 branches served the High Streets of the country.

At that time it was assumed that any proposed merger within the 'Big Five' group of banks would be frowned upon by the Monopolies Commission. The National Provincial and Westminster had a lot in common. A good working relationship had existed between them and there is no doubt that the benefits of a merger must have been informally discussed at a high level, but were deemed to be wishful thinking. However, the fact of Martin's, a small but prestigious bank, putting itself up for sale in 1967 seemed to trigger off positive action. The merger was proposed and met no opposition from the authorities although a later proposal for the union of Barclays, Lloyds and Martin's was given the thumbs down. Barclays had to be content with absorbing Martin's and Lloyds continued to be a considerable force on their own in the banking world.

The operation whereby the District, National Provincial and the Westminster joined forces was completed in January 1970. The restructured bank comprised eight divisions: domestic banking, related banking services and international banking were the premier divisions, with five other groups – business development, financial control, management services, personnel and premises – in support.

After ten years of operation NatWest produced a balance sheet that looked very healthy indeed, showing deposits of more than £26,000 million and annual profits exceeding £440 million. Less than seven years later, in 1986, their books were even healthier. They had become the first ever British bank to hit the £1 billion mark in profits.

Through the late sixties and seventies the underdeveloped third world countries had received, in what then appeared to be shrewd investment policy, very substantial loans from American and European banks to bolster their shaky economies. The long-term loans were seen as development finance, hopefully intended to advance backward industries and help create a stable balance of trade. It was not long before those same debtors were stretched to pay the interest arising from the unpaid interest on the original capital loan. The next step was that South American countries beset by internal strife, the aftermath of a costly Falklands war, and even a total collapse of the economy in some cases, were quite unable to return any payments at all. Massive debts running into billions of pounds would have to be written off. Major banks on both sides of the Atlantic faced losses that, if not crippling, were certainly punishing. It is an example of NatWest's foresight that its international board had reduced their commitment while other banking houses were still pouring hundreds of millions into a hole they still hoped, vainly, to plug. A sign of NatWest capital solidity came in June of 1987 when they announced they were setting aside a sum of £466 million to cover their overseas loan deficits, and this in addition to that already put aside.

In the seventies the London public, used to monolithic buildings rising on old bomb sites, became quite excited at the opportunity

A 600-foot tribute to finance. The
NatWest tower in the City of London.
Watercolour, 22" × 15"

given them of viewing NatWest's new building rising,
appropriately, on its site in Old Broad Street immediately adjacent
to where in 1866 the National Provincial Bank purchased the
Flower Pot tavern and had the architect John Gibson build their new
headquarters. That classical piece of Victorian architecture is still
there today, the oldest of NatWest's banks in the City of London.
Gibson had his problems. 'Ancient Lights', that old established
right of property owners to protect their outlook, was a source of
constant objections to his early designs and he had to satisfy every

complaint – which were manifold. A hundred years later, and justifiably, neighbours still weighed in with their protective weapon of Ancient Lights, which is why you now see a soaring 600-foot tower of gleaming steel and glass. Today's architect, Robert Seifert, was not just trying to reach the stars, merely getting all the required thousands of square feet into the limited space available (the City of London is still only *one* square mile remember) and to keep within the constraints imposed by others' demand for light.

Her Majesty the Queen opened the new international headquarters on 11 June 1981, and the NatWest building now dominates the city skyline east of St Paul's. I am a constant critic of the slab-sided concrete pillars that mutilate the one-time beauty of our capital but have to admit that NatWest Tower is certainly not high-rise simply for the sake of it. It does have a stark, clean elegance about it, it is one high-rise that has risen with grace.

Whilst this exciting building was nearing completion NatWest created further excitement when, breaking through old barriers of tradition and prejudice, they appointed a woman to a senior post. Miss Eileen Cullen became Secretary of the Bank, the first woman ever to hold such an appointment in England. The long-held bastions of chauvinism are cracking!

NatWest chairman Robin Leigh-Pemberton echoed the concern of his banking forebears when in an address he stated that they 'had a duty to contribute to the quality of life of our society'. Well, without a doubt branch managers have become less forbidding and more human towards the more humble customer. That chairman was later given the position of Governor of the Bank of England, the first clearing banker to be so appointed.

Lord Boardman, the present chairman, heads a highly professional team that looks after 6.9 million current accounts, and almost £5 billion-worth of mortgages on the home market. Its foreign acquisitions and subsidiaries are worldwide, with transatlantic success crowned by the takeover in 1979 of the National Bank of North America. Three centuries ago, when they still laboured under the title of moneylenders rather than bankers, critics and customers would not have seen that eventual three-way merger as being particularly holy. But today it has certainly become an established, successful and profitable trinity.

Acorns

Through the previous pages we have met some pretty big companies. For myself a most fascinating part was tracing back their early beginnings – from the oak to the acorn so to speak.

Space does not permit the inclusion of many of the current contemporary 'acorns' of industry. But of the many with ambition and drive and faith in themselves I include just two who portray those traits necessary (next to fickle ladyluck) for success.

A. & A. SPRINKLERS

Even in the ideal society, without war and without natural hazards such as flood, there is always that most fearful danger of Fire – so often caused by our own mistakes or negligence. A statistic table drawn up between the years 1973/85 shows an average of more than 367,000 fires per year. More than a thousand a day! *Fatalities* from fire over that same period were *10,605*. Non-fatal injuries were 88,500. Statistics that are soberly shocking. Among the many regulations that exist, the Fire Precautions Act 1971 (reinforced later with the Fire Precautions Act 1976) was the first to really give authorities teeth to enforce some long overdue fire prevention action. Of the many precautionary and preventative measures that factories, hotels and public buildings were obliged to consider, a water sprinkler system was deemed (and still is) to be the most effective.

It was sprinkler systems that Tony Murphy, made redundant in October 1969, knew something about, and so it was with sprinkler systems that Tony went into business on his own account. It was the classic story, not from rags to riches, but from sudden undeserved misfortune to a flourishing and expanding business.

Tony's wife Peggy took a job while her husband got a starting base established. With long working hours, seven days a week, selling, costing and installing the systems, it needed another to attend to the secretarial and administration work.

That became Peggy's chore after her normal working hours. Oh yes, there were two young children to take care of as well. Working from home cut the overheads of course. Wages? There were none. Peggy's salary kept them until the business moved into the profit sector (just).

Economical it may have been, but as Tony's selling tactics produced more and more results, the simple home base didn't answer production demands and eventually a small factory unit was acquired with a handful of employees. Their own production plant drew the need for welding facilities and a separate company was registered for this purpose with another family member becoming M.D.

With the beginning of expansion Peggy Murphy resigned her Civil Service employment to become full time partner in A & A Sprinklers Ltd. Everything looked set for an ongoing and prosperous future, but storm clouds were just around the corner. It was the mid-seventies and the company was approaching one of those downward financial spirals that seemed to be a regular feature throughout the whole decade. This gave the new welding company problems with cash flow. The parent Sprinkler Company had guaranteed its overdraft.

Their bank, after altering the terms of the guarantee only four weeks before, now called in the overdrafts of both companies. A harrowing experience – the bank put in a Receiver, which action, with the inevitable stigma attached, did nothing to improve matters, but the company was one of the very few which survived receivership. When improvement did come, after another three years, it was due to the guts and determination of the Murphys *not* to be another casualty (and there were many through that period) of the financial squeeze.

A third company set up under their umbrella, A & A Fire Protection Ltd, in 1974, had weathered the storm well and the resiliant success of this company was a great help. Its hard core of servicing and maintenance (possessing its own team of trained service engineers) had continued to flourish where new production and installation had suffered. It was the policy of not having all the eggs in one basket that paid off at the right time. Mindful of this the Murphys set up yet another company in 1984. The industry of Fire Prevention and Servicing was at that time somewhat fragmented. Scores of differing yet necessary pieces of equipment, systems, tools and various aids to Fire Safety were being manufactured by different firms. Sales and distribution rested, haphazardly, on individual practice and policy.

A & A Distribution Ltd, operates not only an efficient distribution service to all the A & A Companies but right through the trade and more recently to the construction industry.

In 1986, mindful of limitations in the parent company operating solely from Scotland, A & A Sprinklers (Midlands) Ltd was set up in Staffordshire. That success is marked by the search now on for larger premises, and watch it you Sassenachs – the Scottish-based Irish firefighters have now stretched their ambitions to London. It's the inevitable move isn't it? A company operating national coverage with production, sales, servicing and maintenance just has to have a capital base.

SKELETAL REMAINS OF AN OIL
PLATFORM ATTACKED BY FIRE
Oil and gas platforms at sea are the
most terrifying potential fire hazards.
The sophisticated systems installed
by A & A Sprinklers reduce the risk
and offer the surest fire-fighting
methods available.
Watercolour and acrylic, 15"x22"

Presently the A & A group of companies employs a total of 60
people in Scotland and England.

When you look back through this book and see what such
companies as Rolls-Royce, Howson Algraphy, ICI, and BP have
achieved over the last fifty years it needs no great stretch of
imagination to see A & A Sprinklers' acorn producing its mighty
oak tree!

GEORGE JOWITT & SONS

There's an area of moorland outside Sheffield that is still scattered with legacies of the Victorian industrial age. Scores of circular quarried sandstone wheels that the layman might assume to be old mill wheels lie neglected and weather beaten on the Yorkshire turf. But the only mills these wheels served were of the 'dark satanic' variety. They are old grinding wheels. Grinders that in their day did their job in the best fashion available. They sharpened the tools with a colourful array of flashing sparks but they also caused disease.

From the wearing face of every wheel, silica dust filled the atmosphere, and in those days when face masks were not even thought of, silica dust meant silicosis. Grinding operatives were guaranteed an early demise – in their 40s – from silicosis.

The industry recognised a desperate need for a better, man made, grinding wheel – as much for improved efficiency as to counter the health hazard. A penknife blade grinder supplied the answer in 1907. George Jowitt's experiments with his first 'artificial' wheel laid the foundations for the present company.

George the father and George the son produced a much improved grinding wheel, which, made in the evening and sold to the factories in the lunch hour, gave them the encouragement in 1919 to start a new business. A rented shop in Sheffield for home production was followed with an American sales agency. When the younger Jowitt took over the business he had obviously inherited all the father's drive and inventiveness. With the introduction of bakelite bonded abrasives Jowitt's reputation in industry soared and a vast sales field opened up.

The Rodgers family of Philadelphia joined forces in 1951 to open the new Jowitt and Rodgers production plant. In 1963 a third manufacturing plant was established in Holland at Best near Eindhoven supplying both Eastern and Western Europe.

VICTORIAN DARK SATANIC MILLS

From the wearing face of every grinding wheel silica dust filled the atmosphere. In those days when face masks were not even thought of, silica dust meant silicosis.

Scenes such as this are now a thing of the past thanks to George Jowitt & Sons.

Watercolour and acrylic, 15"x22"

By 1982 the UK company had outgrown its base and a new, purpose-built factory, with 'garden location' opened at Dronfield, outside Sheffield. Today, grinding has become a hi-tech, precision part of machine production.

Jowitt's wheels, discs, cylinders and segments are in use in virtually every industry throughout Britain and overseas. Grinding and cutting metallic and non-metallic surfaces, mild steel, nickel manganese and magnetic steels, as well as ceramics, all finished to the strictest of tolerances to a fine degree that would have been impossible in the days when George the senior was sharpening pen knife blades.

Jowitt's new factory is a shining example of efficient 20th century technology. All the plant and machinery is modern and sophisticated. They now have their own resin bond production plant. The quality of the 'grain'* is laboratory controlled.

*'grain' is the crushed silicon carbide and aluminium oxide that is the main constituent before 'bonding and baking'.

Computers monitor production and record customer requirements – and yet every item is hand-made!

Like one of their famous customers, Rolls-Royce, the decision was made long ago that to ensure absolute quality, each grinding wheel or segment would be produced by hand. Whether it's a huge turbine blade for British Aerospace, automotive valves or a high speed precision drill that needs to be worked on, the appropriate abrasive item is the final product of human hand and eye.

That this outlook of 'handmade is best' has paid off in such a highly automated age is due largely to the attendant attitude of 'the customer comes first' on the part not only of the management, but of the whole staff.

I tried to extract a few 'personality' stories when I spoke to Jowitts, but they shied away from any individual image projection. Although they have grown they are still a family business, and the 'family' policy extends to their staff.

I met Mrs Elsie Orme, the Company Secretary, sister to George Alan Jowitt, the managing director. My suggestion that her own feminine character qualities added an extra strength to those managerial ones already so obvious in the running of the company was denied. Elsie said, she did this responsible job to the best of her ability and she also happened to be one of the Jowitt family, working with her brother, the third generation George. The company was not eagerly seeking any media exposure. They had a lot of customers – from aircraft and car production giants to the smallest, specialist, precision engineer – and each and everyone came first.

A small British firm with a big future. Present success due to enterprise of the past and its present enterprise assuring success for the future.

In the Picture

The companies in this book have two things in common: they are all successful enterprises in their own special fields, and they all joined the Confederation of British Industry.
The CBI is also a success in its own right – widely acknowledged to be 'Britain's Business Voice'. Companies which together employ about half of the nation's workforce are enjoying the benefits of CBI membership. More than 250,000 firms, public and private, large and small, all feel the need to speak with a single, powerful voice on issues that affect the United Kingdom's prosperity.

Members fund the CBI to give it independence, and its voice is given authority by widespread consultations among them. Some 2,500 businessmen and women have active roles nationwide in the CBI's thirteen Regional Councils, in the Smaller Firms Council and many specialist committees and working parties. The solutions to business problems that they formulate go forward to the central Council of some 400 senior industrialists who, with specialist advice from staff, agree the policies that will promote the nation's wealth and efficiency into the 21st century.

Promoting the importance of wealth creation to the country is one of the major roles of the CBI. This can be achieved only by the continuing success of enterprises such as the ones pictured here, and by raising the public's awareness of them. That is the purpose of this book.

Confederation of British Industry
Centre Point
103 New Oxford Street
London WC1A 1DU
Tel: 01-379 7400

Overleaf
THE NABORS RIG
The first oil production platform in
the Arctic at Prudhoe Bay, 300 miles
inside the Arctic Circle.
Oil on Canvas, 28"x36"

ben maile

CBI OFFICES

Headquarters
Centre Point, 103 New Oxford Street, London WC1A 1DU
Telephone: 01 379 7400, Telex: 21332
Facsimile: 01 240 1578

The English Regions

Eastern
14 Union Road
Cambridge CB2 1HE
Telephone: 0223 65636
Regional Director:
Arthur Wilman

East Midlands
17 St Wilfred Square
Calverton
Nottingham NG14 6FP
Telephone: 0602 653311
Regional Director:
Ken Barnes

London
Centre Point
103 New Oxford Street
London WC1A 1DU
Telephone: 01 379 7400
Regional Director:
Peter Waine

Northern
15 Grey Street
Newcastle-upon-Tyne
NE1 6EE
Telephone: 091 232 1644
Regional Director:
Arthur Foord

North Western
Emerson House
Albert Street
Eccles
Manchester M30 0LT
Telephone: 061 707 2190
Regional Director:
Andrew Toop

Southern
Bank Chambers
10a Hart Street
Henley-on-Thames
Oxfordshire RG9 2AU
Telephone: 0491 576810
Regional Director:
Richard Griffiths

South Eastern
Tubs Hill House
London Road
Sevenoaks
Kent TN13 1BX
Telephone: 0732 454040
Regional Director:
Geoffrey Warr

South Western
8/10 Whiteladies Road
Bristol BS8 1NZ
Telephone: 0272 737065
Regional Director:
Chris Curtis

West Midlands
Hagley House
Hagley Road
Edgbaston
Birmingham B16 8PS
Telephone: 021 454 7991
Regional Director:
John Gunn

Yorkshire & Humberside
Arndale House
Station Road
Crossgates
Leeds LS15 8EU
Telephone: 0532 644242
Regional Director:
Brian Bigley

Northern Ireland
Fanum House
108 Great Victoria Street
Belfast BT2 7PD
Telephone: 0232 226658
Director: Alasdair
          MacLaughlin

Scotland
Beresford House
5 Claremont Terrace
Glasgow G3 7XT
Telephone: 041 332 8661
Director: John Davidson

Wales
Pearl Assurance House
Greyfriars Road
Cardiff CF1 3JR
Telephone: 0222 32536
Director: Ian Kelsall

Brussels
40 Rue Joseph II
Bte 14, B-1040
Brussels
Belgium
Telephone:
(010 322) 231 04 65
(010 322 231 05 73)

CBI – active in...

Company & Environmental Affairs
Company law
Competition policy
Government contracts
Corporate responsibilities
Commercial law
Consumer affairs
Technical legislation
Environmental policy
Water supply
Pollution
Minerals and land use

Economic
Economic and financial policy
Liaison with the City
Industrial policy, including regional policy and activities of the
    Department of Industry
Taxation policy
Rating and local authority finance
Accounting standards
Economic situation and forecasting
Industrial Trends and Distributive Trades Surveys
Statistics
NEDC and Economic Development Councils
Government grants advice

Education, Training and Technology
Eudcation and training policy
Production efficiency
Quality, standards, design
Marketing
Research and technology
Biotechnology
Technical barriers to trade
Links between business and schools, universities, polytechnics
    and colleges
Energy policy
Transport policy
Information technology

Employment Affairs
Industrial relations
Pay and benefits
Unemployment
Manpower and working practices
Pensions
Social security
Employment information/Pay Databank
Employment law
Employee relations
Equal opportunities
Occupational health and safety
International labour matters
EC employment policies

Information
Relations with Press, radio and television, public and Parliament
Publications
Audio-visual and video production
CBI News magazine
Publicity activities
Library services

International Affairs
Overseas trade policy
European Community policy
International relations
Trading conditions and opportunities in individual countries
Overseas investment
Export promotion policy and export credits
Development aid

Regional and Smaller Firms
CBI in the Regions
Regional Councils and members' groups
Consultation with membership
All aspects of CBI's activites dealing with smaller firms
Impact of legislation, taxation, industrial strategy and regional,
    economic and financial policy on smaller firms

*Specialists covering all these subjects are
available to help members.*